8

The Perfect Plan

The Story That Reveals the Secret of the World's Elite Sales and Marketing Teams

Donald W. Barden

First Edition

WestBow
PRESS
A DIVISION OF THOMAS NELSON

WestBow Press books may be ordered through booksellers or by contacting:

WestBow Press
A Division of Thomas Nelson
1663 Liberty Drive
Bloomington, IN 47403
www.westbowpress.com
1-(866) 928-1240

ISBN: 978-1-4497-6563-7 (hc)
ISBN: 978-1-4497-6564-4 (sc)
ISBN: 978-1-4497-6565-1 (e)

Library of Congress Control Number: 2012916363

Printed in the United States of America

WestBow Press rev. date: 10/03/2012

Table of Contents

To Lisa and the Boys

Special Thanks to Indiana, Kansas and Canada

The Elite 1% (*noun*) e·lite one per·cent [ih-**leet** wuhn per-**sent**]

1. (*often used with a plural verb*) the choice or best of anything considered collectively, as of a group or class of persons.

2. (*used with a plural verb*) the best of the best persons of the highest class: *Only the elite were there.*

3. a tip of the classical organizational bell curve, the pinnacle of an organizations performers.

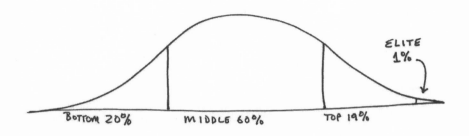

4. An individual or group of persons that is so good, others begin to ask "why?"

5. Those typically ignored by management because there seems to be no reasonable explanation for their excellence.

6. Those who have a plan.

7. Those who change the world.

What others are saying about The Perfect Plan

"In my 14 years of operating The Brain Trust, we have now seen over 150 speakers. Don's presentation on The Perfect Plan was easily in our top 3 presentations of all time.

The Perfect Plan is the highest value I have ever seen related to the field of best practices in selling. As a matter of fact, one of our members commented after the presentation that this was more than about selling . . . it was really about leadership at the highest level."

Tom Cramer—CEO
The Brain Trust

"I have known Don Barden for over 12 years. He has never failed to deliver on any of his commitments. It is rare when you can say this about anyone in today's markets. He is someone I trust and always does the right, moral, and ethical thing for me and those he serves.

Don throws himself passionately into everything he does. Whether it is his family, his faith, his business, or even his health, Don gives 100% effort to achieve maximum outcomes. I admire and respect him both personally and professionally, and have learned many valuable lessons from him throughout the years.

The Perfect Plan is an example of the thoughtful focus he is capable of creating and communicating that hits home with all audiences. Whether you are in the financial industry or not, everyone can benefit from the lessons learned from The Perfect Plan.

James "J" Laschinger
Senior Vice President
Alliant Retirement Services

"If Wall Street would really listen, the Perfect Plan would change their world . . . The impact it has had on our firm is immeasurable."

Scott Keller, CFA
Principal
The Henssler Financial Group

"Don came in to our school and spoke to the leaders and teachers about the Perfect Plan. We were all blown away with what we learned in just a single day."

Trey Arnett
Development Chair and Head of Middle School
Mount Pisgah Christian School

"I've known Don for the past few years and I've always been aware of his success, but hearing him go through The Perfect Plan pulled my attention away from how he's become successful and made me more aware of how everyone he works with is successful. He simply makes you better."

Mark Conroy—Regional Vice President

"There is a reason why we see $1billion in sales, and the Perfect Plan is it!"

James Gilligan
Senior Sales and Marketing Director
OneAmerica Financial Partners

"I have just gotten back to my desk because of the number of people that have stopped me to declare Don's impact on their life today, and have asked when he can come back a share more of the story. Don has many very special gifts and God is working miracles in and through these gifts. Thank you for sharing the "Perfect Plan" with our team today. Wow!"

David Mann, President
Strong Rock Christian School

After ten years of fear-based marketing, the clarity on the mechanics of human communication in the Perfect Plan turned my personal and professional communications upside down. The result is an approach that is as calming for someone who hates "hunting" as it is for my prospects and my family. They now all receive a message of gratitude, key information, and ease of doing business. I look forward to years of rewarding professional relationships, . . . and a happy wife & kid!

Michael Case Smith
Retirement Plan Advisor
Jacksonville, Florida

"This is so exciting—I now see our people focused on the "joy" and the "pleasure" of our business!"

Janet Piper
Senior VP
CCCi

"Thank you for the Perfect Plan training over the years. It's changed the way we interact with the world!"

Chris Burr
Financial Advisor—Delray Beach
APA

"The Perfect Plan is the missing piece of the puzzle. The Perfect Plan has allowed us into a different context by revealing the act of "corporate generosity" from organizations offering retirement plans to their employees. It has helped us work closer with plan participants to redefine their retirement in a much more meaningful & achievable way.

As a practitioner managing dozens of retirement plans, having more meaningful conversations with plan sponsors and their participants is everything. The Perfect Plan has allowed us to connect with our clients and prospects at a different level, which in turn has made a tremendous impact to our business and the clients we serve. Thank you Don!"

Alvaro A. Galvis, CFM, CRPC(r),CRPS(r)
Vice President
Wealth Management Advisor
International Financial Advisor
The MG Group

Introduction

The Perfect Plan started out as a simple hypothesis that rattled around in my mind through the late hours of a summer night.

It began on the beach with 4th of July fireworks and continued while I scribbled on napkins and loose scraps of paper as I watched my children play.

It was a theory—an idea that made complete sense in my mind, and when written out, looked even better on paper. It was one of those ideas that seemed too good to be true.

It looked so great because it was immensely radical yet brilliantly simple. I wanted to know if it could actually work in real life. Could it live up to the marketing potential that seemed obvious to me? And if it worked in actual practice, then to what lengths could it go? The potential impact was huge.

Then I wondered if I had stumbled upon something new and innovative, or was it an age old secret. My immediate reaction was, "Of course it's not new, but why would it be a secret?"

It seemed odd that I had never heard of it before, and the simplicity of the Plan made me wonder why. Was it too complex? It didn't appear to be . . . a little maybe, but nothing a person with commitment, some right side brain activity, plenty of ethics, and a lot of character couldn't achieve its full potential.

So I set out to prove my hypothesis true, because ultimately, that is all that matters. A theory on paper is intriguing, but it is worthless if only an idea. From there, the questions became obvious. Can it be proven and can it be replicated? That is where the real impact lies, and that is the secret to it all.

So, for the next 10 years, I and a team of brilliant men and women set out to discover if the Perfect Plan was actually "perfect" or not. We certainly learned a lot, but one thing that stood out to us almost immediately was that our theory is true—it was the secret practice of the Top 1% of the world's sales and marketing teams. It was they who consistently defied all traditional standards of marketing, behavioral strategy, and business logic, and they who became the elite in their fields.

It was there, and in the end we found the beginning.

We discovered the Perfect Plan.

Chapter 1

The Unfair Advantage

All anyone wants in life is an advantage—an unfair advantage, to be precise.

That's what the Perfect Plan was and is, an unfair advantage.

Simply put, the Perfect Plan is the secret formula of the world's top sales and marketing professionals. It doesn't matter what they are selling . . . the Perfect Plan is there. From products to policy, from self-esteem to relationships, everyone is selling something, and the Perfect Plan is the key to the elite level of success. We discovered its source, studied its impact, reverse engineered its design, and with critical and controlled trials, proved it to be true. It was the key to success we all knew was there, but now it became real.

As I mentioned, it all began on July 4th, 2000. That was a great day for everyone. America was celebrating its 224th year of independence, the sun was shining on the beach, and the world hadn't ended earlier that year in any of the dreaded Y2K predictions. It was that day on the beach that I had sunk deep into thought when the idea presented itself to me.

That's where it all began. It was the point where the original hypothesis for the Perfect Plan found its legs. It was one of those moments when your mind is somewhere your body is not, and in that mystic moment, the idea appeared. It was so strong and so clear that I knew then and there it was true. I also knew that proving it would be difficult, but possible. Looking back on that day, I would never have guessed where the path to proving it would take me or how many incredible people I would come to meet. It became a journey that led me around the world to befriend and work with some of the greatest people on earth.

It was a beautiful evening on the beach, where the kids were preparing to shoot fireworks at sunset. Our family has made Amelia Island our 4th of July tradition and I look forward to it every year. Thousands of people line the beach at sunset, where you can see and feel the fireworks for miles on end. The beach becomes a dreamland of lights that draws you in and envelops you in bursts of colors and noise. You can see the fireworks from Georgia all the way down to Jacksonville and Ponte Vedra. The fireworks on Amelia Island are "participatory" which means you become part of the show. Not only do you shoot your own fireworks, but they seem to burst around you in a dream like state, and that lends to an even more patriotic atmosphere, as everyone comes together to wish America the happiest of birthdays. It is always special, and it takes you back in time to a place when things meant more and America was a little more "real."

I watched the children play on the beach and enjoyed the feeling of "living inside" the fireworks. That is when I realized something different was happening. I was full of special memories and typical thoughts of 4th of July sentiments when my mind began to drift someplace different. I began to lose the sense and smell of the ocean mixing with the sulfur residue of the fireworks and began to hear a conversation brewing in my head. For the strangest reason, I was not able to shake it. My mind seemed to fixate on the thought and then wandered quickly to a sense of wonderment. It was a silly feeling at first, but I began to rationalize the thought into a logical question of "what if?"

So there it was . . . a seemingly perfect idea, a working hypothesis, but what if it was true?

It was one of those moments when I felt like jumping up and down, but my family was there, including my 3 boys, my wife, her sister, half a dozen of my nieces and nephews, plus whoever else had wandered over that night. Jumping up and down like a giddy schoolboy did not seem to be the best plan to get people to take me seriously.

So, late that night after everyone else had crashed for the evening, I began to write it all down. I was used to writing late at night, because I had just finished my Master's degree and was well entrenched in my doctoral work. Since I had 3 small children and a full-time career, I rarely began my academic studies until long after sundown, so staying up late with a laptop was nothing unusual. My wife likes to say that I am the only person she ever met who wrote such deep and profound work—she was being a bit facetious perhaps—while wearing an old pair of SpongeBob SquarePants PJ's—a Father's Day gift my boys had given me a few years before. I was working on my PhD and studying the effects of immigration on long-term pension liabilities absorbed in Europe and the United Kingdom. Exciting stuff, eh? I don't think so either. Still, it set the stage for what was to come.

As far as academics goes, I had just about learned all there was regarding finance and economics. I was moving away from the traditional core curriculums and began to go deep into the minds of human behavior. I had reached a place where the academics of economics became frail and the logic a bit weathered. I was becoming bored with the concept of sterile financial decisions.

I quickly came to believe that economics, finance, and accounting were just historical truths built on the records of the past. They rarely looked with any credible forethought into the future and certainly never joined itself to any real risk. That's where the Harry Truman joke originated about the two-handed economist. He once stated that all he wanted was a one-handed economist, because all of his economic advisors kept referring to their "two hands." President Truman complained that everything they told him went something like this: "Well, Mr. President, on one hand, it could be this, and on the other hand, it could be something completely different." It was a classical economic explanation, always claiming the only way to know the next logical step was to understand the steps of the past and previous situations. They would then toss out disclaimers regarding other possible outcomes, admitting, albeit reluctantly, that human nature has a penchant for changing the direction of its own future.

It is a subtle admission that they really don't have very much understanding of the things to come, but know a ton about the past. To their credit, most economists do acknowledge one significant truth: we are all free thinkers, and at any time, we might just forget where we have been and wander off into a new and 'unpredictable' path. That's the point where I became bored and started looking for a deeper understanding of economics and finance—something beyond the boundaries of Wall Street, stocks, bonds, pensions, and above all, 'classical economics.'

However you look at it, I was getting bored and was beginning to look for something deeper. That's why that night on the beach came to mean so much to me. When the original hypothesis came, it was more than a great idea; it was the key to unlocking the next step in my own academic evolution and the start of something wonderful.

Earlier in that year, I was asked to write a paper about the person I felt was the world's leading CEO. It was an opinion paper only, not meant to create any traction. Nevertheless, it planted some purposeful seeds in my mind. That night, on the 4th of July, I found it strange when that particular paper came rushing back to the forefront of my mind. Suddenly, it all became clear. There were no coincidences.

The idea I wrote down that night was a fictional account of what I was convinced was true. I did it this way because I felt people wouldn't believe it until it had been proven. I hoped that, as a metaphor, it might stand a chance of gaining traction and recognition. I know that's not the best way, but I wanted to tell the world as soon as possible, even if it meant releasing it before I proved it to be true. It seemed like the best way at the time, and that's where all the logical thoughts in my head were pointing me. Eventually, however, I realized that it was best to wait and follow the protocols necessary for scientific proof. I had a legitimate hypothesis and the ability to prove it, so that is what I needed to do. Fortunately, the days, weeks and years ahead would lend themselves to the proof, and in the end, I was able to answer the question of its validity with 100% confidence.

Yes, it was true.

What began as a question in my subconscious, quickly developed into something special from the very beginning. As the Perfect Plan was revealed to my understanding, I took a deep breath and exhaled. I knew it was good, but I wanted to test and retest it until there was no doubt in anyone's mind.

What we discovered was the method and formula to a practice that would ultimately take me and my team back over a 5,000 year journey of research and study as we sought to prove its validity. From Eastern Europe to Mexico, from the United States to India, we checked and rechecked until there was nothing else we could do.

We stripped out the little nuances of culture, rolled it through history and used a variety of comparative analyses, the results of which no one could have guessed at in the beginning. We also self-injected the study, as most mad scientists ultimately do, and found that it worked just as well on our own group as it did on all others combined.

It was true, it was pure, and it really was perfect.

10 years later when it was all done, our research and testing held a sense of 'completeness' about the truth of the Perfect Plan. That is when we began taking a look back across the scope of what we had learned.

As the Perfect Plan revealed itself, we found that several other lessons existed and were woven into the end product. These lessons were the fiber that allowed success to come, but unlike the final product, they could stand alone on their own merits, totally independent of each other. They were principles of success that, on the surface, seemed easy to understand, but were often lost in the shadows of a busy life. There was probably a time in each of our lives when these values had been taught to us and we understood them, but as we grew and matured, they became lost in our ambitions and desires. Everyone hears them taught as a child, some more than others, but these principles have been part of our lives since those very early days.

As my team looked across the room and smiled, we began to put the puzzle pieces together. The simplicity of the principles that were woven into the Perfect Plan was astonishing, but it quickly became clear to us that it was not necessarily the ingredients that made the Plan special. *It was the order in which they built upon each other that drove the Plan forward.* It was the purity of a few organized sequences that opened our minds and touched our hearts to the power it held.

As you begin to explore the truths of the Perfect Plan with me, we will witness what they can do, and in the end, you will find the beginning. It will be the start of something so perfect that you will be amazed at the future you discover and the Plan that lies before you.

But what would you do with the Perfect Plan? What do you do when you discover the formula that unlocks the mystery as to why the Top 1% of people throughout history have been so excellent at what they do? What happens when you discover a group of people whose performance is so good that they are literally off any measurable chart? What happens when seemingly every effort to track their success is for naught, because outsiders get so caught up in the results that they forget to ask how or why?

The Perfect Plan is the simple reason why the Top 1% of the world's sales, marketing, political, religious, and business people become successful. It is the one thing that makes 'the best' better than anyone else—even in relationships, marriages, and children. The Perfect Plan lays the steps to success with a foundation so strong, that when sincerely applied and executed, the 'close' rate is close to 95%. It pushes the perceived boundaries by allowing an uncontained growth rate of over 300% per year! Even better, when properly applied, people are moved, policies are set, sales are closed, and markets are leveraged.

It is simple and powerful. So much so that when we came to realize that the original hypothesis was proven true, we wanted to tell the world. It was exciting, but it was 10 years later when it all began to make sense.

Leveraging the Unfair Advantage

$450,000,000.00.

That's a lot of money—in anyone's book. It seemed even more so to me when the decision of how the client would spend it hinged on a single presentation that would last no more than 45 minutes. On top of the $450 million, another $90 million would be spent with the winner of the contract each year. I wanted this contract—badly, but I wasn't the only one in the running for it. I knew better, and my own experiences had taught me that the final decision would come down to a single moment in time, but what would be the deciding factor?

- ❖ Would a complicated set of variables that uses multiple logarithms be employed to deduce which firm would be best suitable to win the deal, or would it be a gut feeling?

- ❖ Would the buying committee follow a time tested series of principles that have been passed down from generation to generation, or would a simple pretty smile tip the scales in our favor?

- ❖ Would they decide based on their collective academic and business experience, or would it come down to a beauty contest of who simply 'looks' like the deserving candidate?

In the moments leading up to such a presentation, these are the thoughts that usually flash through the minds of the hopefuls, sounding like a jackhammer pounding on their skulls and eroding away at their confidence. That's where the best start to prevail, because they know that 'hope' is not a strategy. We had a plan. We were the best, and we knew it.

It is not from pride or ego that I believe this. Thanks to our work on The Perfect Plan, we really were the best. We had led the industry for years and broken every record in the books. We managed to win some of the most prestigious and sought after accounts in the country, so why should this one be any different? For weeks, we had been practicing and prepping for this moment, and we knew everyone's move before they had even thought about it themselves. We were the best trained, best educated, and best prepared team in the country. We were ready.

On this particularly sunny day in Southern California, we were set to make our presentation and land this 450 million dollar deal, but there was only one seemingly irritating snag. We drew the dreaded position of being the first of the three finalists to present. When all the 'marbles' are at stake, most large clients will narrow their search down to the top three contenders for a final presentation. They usually enforce strict rules of engagement and ask you to keep your presentation to 45 minutes which will then be followed by an extra 10 minutes of a Q&A session.

Most good teams will put in over 80 hours of intense preparation for an account like this, trying to boil it all down to a presentation of less than one hour. In contrast, our team spent over 200 hours on this particular client, including design, creativity, style, R&D, and even a little covert guerilla action. So while being first was never the best pole position, it didn't bother us in the least.

Our team spent the day before our presentation at a luxury hotel in the same city as the client. This is customary for several reasons. We needed everyone rested and relaxed within the same time zone as the client, but we also wanted everyone involved in the presentation to feel good about themselves and about how much their work meant to our organization.

It was a little token of our appreciation that worked in a variety of ways. The team members who worked the hardest felt a little appreciation and being pampered in the hotel helped them to mentally prepare for the expectations of the client. We always felt that if we immersed ourselves into someone else's service (a 5 star resort), then we would take that attitude of servitude into our presentation. If we 'lived' it, we knew we could 'deliver' it. We certainly wanted the best for the client . . . and a little bit of fun for ourselves.

We spent the afternoon in our prep area, running through mock ups of the presentation room, the gender mixes, and even seating arrangements for the following day. It was always casual and never scripted, but certainly 100% rehearsed. All the details were discussed. We decided who should enter the room first and who should target who with small talk. We knew the committee members lives, personal styles, and predictable natures with CIA type precision. We even set the ground rules for our dress code and discussed how someone should sit during the presentation. We decided how, and if, the women on our team should carry purses into the meeting, even down to which shoulder they would carry it on. It might sound silly to some, but big decisions are made from the smallest of actions, and we wanted it to be perfect, and that is never easy.

As a long standing tradition, just before we actually began the last day of practice for the big presentation, I would always tell my team the story of how I once saw a woman's career crash for something so insignificant, that, to this day, she still doesn't know how it happened.

The story went like this:

As a younger man just finishing up with my undergraduate degree, I was hunting around for a 'real' job. As a very poor college kid with one month to go before graduation, I was perfectly content in my role at the time. But in the back of my mind, I knew I needed to move on to fulfill my career aspirations. While finishing school, I had the incredibly stupid job of chasing shoplifters out of a large—very large, actually—downtown department store. I generally had 50 to 100 yards to catch said culprit, knock them down, and wait for the police to show up. And that's where the stupid part kicked in. What do you do in the 30 seconds after you knock them down and before the police get there? Pray!

There was a huge benefit to the job that kept me from quitting. I spent the day standing in the woman's cosmetics area located by the store's main front doors—the preferred exit route for most of the petty criminals. So while attentively keeping an eye out for shoplifters, I got to talk with some beautiful girls who worked in the area, making the time pass quickly and pleasantly.

One day just before I graduated and after a 10 hour day on Peachtree Street with another 5 hours in class, I got home to my apartment to find a peculiar message on my answering 'machine' (yes, this predates voice mail, emails, and cell phones). The message was simple. I was to show up at work the next morning in my best suit and tie and be prepared to meet the company's CEO . . . that's all it said! So I rushed to clean my best—and only—suit and ended up staying awake all night with wonderful, but terribly inflated, possibilities floating around in my mind. Would I be made a senior financial trader for the firm, head of new accounts, CFO ... what would it be? I was literally breathless with anticipation.

The next day, I arrived as directed and went straight to the CEO's office. Having never been there before, I was in awe of the mahogany panels, the two secretaries out front, and the CEO's own private waiting room. It was old school New York class at its best. I had no idea why I was there, but I knew it would be great.

After a few moments, the CEO's personal assistant, an elegant older lady, came out to meet me with the Senior Vice President of Security and Safety in tow. I understood why she was there, and I certainly knew who he was, but I had no idea what he wanted with me. They politely took me back to a lovely private parlor room decked out with its own fireplace—*cool, right?*—and began to explain why I had been called in and why that day was the first day I would begin wearing a suit to work for the next 25 years and more. Though I didn't know it at the time, the CEO, who was actually based out of New York City, was contemplating moving their corporate offices to Atlanta and was about to spend 6 months commuting up and down the east coast. They wanted me to be there for him and act as his personal staff aid, which immediately translated to 'driver' in my mind. It was a long way from the CFO job that I was naive enough to dream about, but what the heck, I got to drive a new Mercedes and hang out with a guy who knew more about business and marketing than almost anyone else in the world.

I was in, and loving it.

I learned a lot over the 6 months he and I were together, and he always treated me with great respect. To him, I was a young, eager kid who just graduated from college and was looking to find my way in the world, and it didn't hurt that I was the same age as his grandsons. He taught me more in those 6 months than I ever learned in the prior 4 years of college education and would learn over the next 6 years of graduate and post graduate studies. It was great, but there was one particular night in New Orleans that made an impression on me like nothing I had ever seen before.

I had gotten to the point where I was put in charge of his guests and the introductions of people wanting to meet him. Vendors, managers, and even a few famous sales guys would meet me first and before formally being introduced to the boss. It was kind of like meeting royalty, and in the garment business, he was king.

One of his 'royal' traditions was to take a new store's management team out for a huge feast the night before they opened their new location. The team consisted of the store's General Manager, Operations Manager, Human Resource personnel, and of course, all the floor managers. It was always festive and something I really enjoyed watching. That night we had rented out an entire restaurant, famous for its 5 star food and locale. It was an old antebellum home that had been converted into an incredible eating establishment. We had a great time as he toasted their future success. As we finished for the evening and walked out to our car, he was happier than I had ever seen him. He boasted about the quality of the new team and predicted that their sales and numbers would break all the records.

Then it happened.

As we got into our car, he saw something beginning to unfold in the parking lot and asked me not to drive away, but to position our car so we both could watch. I obeyed.

The Operations Manager from the new store had come out of the restaurant and was approaching her car. Everything seemed safe enough, and she followed all of the proper procedures for a young, attractive woman walking by herself at night. She opened the door and started her car without incident. What happened next began the worst moment of her corporate career as she started to back out of a rather odd parking position.

It was actually more than odd. It was impossible. She had, in an obvious hurry to avoid being late to the dinner, wedged her car on to the curb and between a tree, a large dumpster, and several other cars. She had parked so precariously, that she was beyond any hope of a three point "Y" turn. She made over 25 short maneuvers going forward 12 inches, turning the wheel, inching back 12 inches, turning the wheel the other way, forward, back, forward, back—it seemed to last forever. Once she finally got clear, there was a short moment of anticipation that she might bottom out as she came off the curb. She did. With heroic fashion, sparks flew and metal collided with hard Louisiana concrete as her car smashed down off the curb and onto the street. She drove off with an obvious sense of relief, seemingly to think nothing of it—just another New Orleans parking dilemma solved.

While she thought nothing of it, the boss thought a lot about it.

As we sat in relative silence, watching her drive off under the streetlights, the CEO spoke with an air of disappointment about a decision I never saw coming. "That's a shame," he said softly.

"Yeah," I replied, thinking about the damage to her car.

"I hate to see such a bright young woman ruin her career over something as silly as parking a car," he continued.

I blinked, bewildered. "What do you mean? Was that a company car?"

"No," he said with a slight but sad laugh. "The truth is simple here kid. How can I ever trust her to run one of my stores, if she can't even park a car the right way?"

I turned around, shocked. "Are you telling me that just because she got herself stuck and had a tough time backing out, her career is ruined?"

"That's exactly what I am saying." His tone left no doubt to his seriousness. "You see son, it is the little things that count and even the smaller things that make the biggest impressions, but don't worry . . . she's a sharp girl, and I am sure someone else will hire her."

Wow, and she never even knew it.

I tell this story to all of my teams before every meeting. It's the little things that can swing a sale, so on a $450 million dollar deal we had better get it right. All of the study, R&D, and training mean nothing if the clients become distracted by something so simple, that their decision is based on a vague impression instead of your work, skill, or talents. The reason we focus on the smallest detail is not because it will win the deal, but to eliminate possible distractions. You never want to create a distraction that takes the client's focus off of the real decision and your ability to present your work. Too many deals are lost for all the wrong reasons—usually because someone got distracted about a minor detail that others thought nothing about.

If you don't believe me and don't understand that it's the little things that make all the difference, you had better stop reading right now, because you have failed to comprehend what the best in the world understand. Details rarely win a deal, but they neutralize the environment so everyone can focus on the important stuff. So if you remember anything from this book, remember this: *If it looks easy, it's not.*

So, almost 20 years after that incident in Louisiana, on that day in Southern California, we were grateful, well educated, and totally prepared to make it look easy. We knew the stakes and we were ready.

Everything went on schedule that day, and we had a perfect delivery. The entrance, the set, the transitions, and the presentation itself were flawless. We were simply great, and it showed.

After we finished, something wonderful happened. The CEO, in a very uncustomary fashion, stood up and came all the way around the boardroom table. I stood at attention and displayed all of the proper courtesies, thinking to hear a routine close to the meeting and a pleasant, "Thank you." But that's not what happened.

As she came close to me, she put out her hand and with a huge smile said the most beautiful words anyone in sales and marketing can ever hope to hear, "Congratulations, you win the deal!"

I hesitated for a moment, not fully grasping what she said, but it was true! We had won the deal—all $450 million of it.

It was uncharacteristic and slightly out of protocol to award any deal so soon, especially without hearing the other two bidders present, but she was convinced that we were the best.

She noted our professionalism and told us that she felt sorry for the other 2 who were still scheduled to present after us. She even went so far as to ask that we return the following Monday to begin the work and even offered to take us to a celebration dinner the following week. It was simply the best feeling in the world—a $450 million dollar win, even after drawing the worst spot of the day! For a moment, a brief feeling of compassion towards our competitors came over me, because I knew that they worked hard too, but in this case, we had worked harder and we knew a few secrets they probably did not.

We all shook hands as we exited, and I told them we were looking forward to seeing them the following week. Their business consultant, a broker who had connected us with the client was ecstatic, and we quickly planned a celebration drink together for that night at the hotel bar before I flew home the next morning. The rest of my team said goodbye and headed toward an executive airport where our corporate G5 airplane was waiting to take them home. I was thrilled to stay behind one more day to debrief with the broker and enjoy a little victory cocktail. What a day!

That evening, I floated out of my room and rushed to the resort's main restaurant and bar for what I figured would be the best post victory dinner of the year. The broker was a good friend of mine, and we had referred business to each other for years. I knew his wife and two wonderful little girls, and I knew he would be just as happy for our team as he would be for anyone else. I hurried to the bar, arriving a few moments before he did. I had in hand my traditional victory drink, what I describe as 'Daddy's Little Helper' (a Gentleman Jack on the rocks with a slight splash of diet cola and a lime, of course). As I took my first wonderful and well deserved sip, it happened.

I looked up and . . .

Well, suffice it to say, I'll finish this story later. What is important here is that the Perfect Plan is not a new innovation. It is something everyone can do in order to gain an *unfair advantage.*

Chapter 2

The Perfect Plan

The Perfect Plan is the hidden secret of history's best and brightest. It is the communication path that helped move the markets that revolutionized the world. It is the simple step to a 95% close ratio in business and a successful life in general.

It's perfect by its very existence, and best of all, it is really good news.

In effect, the Perfect Plan is the result of a collision between 3 *Promises* and 3 *Beliefs*. When a presentation is made, it follows the sequence of the three *Promises*. It is the logical order of things, backed with scientific evidence that proves why it is so effective. We also learned that as these three *Promises* are implemented, an interesting phenomenon occurred. The 'buyer,' or prospect at hand, is bonded with the presenter, clearly understands what's needed, and is relieved at the "ease" from which it flows. But that's not enough. As the Perfect Plan lays the pattern, the buyer will ultimately want to know 'who' you are.

This is when the **3 *Promises*** collide with the **3 *Beliefs*.** The buyer then feels magnetized to bond, understands the value of what you are offering, and glimpses into your forward state of being. Then, and only then, can the person make a decision because 3 *questions* that the buyer asked himself were answered positively in the presentation. They need to know if harmony exists between what's right for them personally, professionally, and in their spirit. If all 3 questions are answered 'yes,' then they have a good decision. But this is where it begins, not where it ends.

The Perfect Plan is not a magical formula or even a tool. It is an extension of *you*. It is ultimately a belief system that is demonstrated in every word, every action, and every thought you make when presenting yourself and your product to a prospect.

Let's take a look at the Perfect Plan in a synopsis form here before getting into a more in-depth explanation.

The Three Promises

The 3 promises of the Plan are rather simple. They are:

1. **Attitude of Gratitude**
2. **Real Education**
3. **Ease of Business**

In that order! The order, we found, is essential to the process. These promises are what you offer to the prospect. They are an expression of what is part of you.

The Three Beliefs

When the 3 promises are presented in perfect order, the prospect will want to know who you are and what you believe . . . your belief system.

The effective belief system for the Perfect Plan is made up of three simple states:

1. **"Create", Don't "Compete"**
2. **Value is Greater than the Cost**
3. **Always "Give Forward"**

This is the 'who' of 'you.' The order of the presentation needs to occur in perfect fashion, but ultimately the prospect wants to know 'who' you are and 'what' you believe.

The Three Questions

Once they know your promises and belief system, they will then ask themselves 3 questions. The answers to these questions will ultimately determine the decision they make. Here they are:

1. **Is this the right decision for me personally?**
2. **Is this the right decision for me professionally?**
3. **Is this the right decision for me spiritually (in my conscience)?**

The Top 1% already know the answers to these questions before even making the presentation to the client. The Top 1% asks these questions on behalf of the client, because their own belief system requires them to be a *servant,* not a marketer or salesman.

Servants actually begin the process by asking themselves, "If I am to serve this person, will it be right for them personally, professionally, and in their spirit? And if so, then and only then, will I present myself to them with an attitude of gratitude, real education, and ease of business—because that's what servants do. Then I will be there for them with a creative spirit and not a competitive attitude. I will have a value greater than the cost, and I will give forward . . . because that's what servants do."

The Top 1% actually turn the entire concept of marketing upside down because they are not in the sales and marketing world at all! They are servants, and that is the most perfect situation to build upon.

Everyone is trying to figure out how the Top 1% sell so much, but, quite frankly, most people miss the entire concept because they are looking at it the wrong way. They are trying to see both sides of a single coin, not realizing that there are *three* sides to it—heads, tails, and "the edge". As with a coin flip, ever so often, it actually lands on its side. Everyone seems to choose just heads or tails, but the Elite 1% know something different. There is more than the buyer and the seller. There is the servant.

The Top 1% become "who" they are because they are *servants*. This attitude along with their *Promises* and *Beliefs* is what affords them the perfect approach that closes so many sales and ultimately influences human behavior.

Over the next few chapters, we will discuss in detail each of these concepts and ideas and how they not only relate to you and your clients, but also the effect they have on each surrounding principle in order to drive the Perfect Plan forward.

As with the process itself, we start where others think it ends—in the mind of the prospect. Only by understanding why a person, or a committee makes their decisions, and what questions they ask of themselves, we can serve them.

Chapter 3

Understanding the Decision Making Process

To better understand how the Top 1% utilizes the Perfect Plan, it is essential to understand how and why people make the decisions they do. Understanding that will help you implement the Perfect Plan in the way it was meant to be used.

In the beginning of our journey, we quickly learned that there are 3 things everyone needs in their lives in order to make good decisions. Decisions have untold ramifications on the future that cannot be charted in advance or predicted with any real degree of certainty. Therefore, decision makers must decide based on certain core principles and innate (gut) feelings.

The Need for *Valuable* Advice

The first is *valuable advice*. I'm talking about the kind your mother and grandmother give you. It's the concepts, ideas, values, and wisdom you take in as a child and build upon as you grow, learn, and mature. It is the sort of thing that you find important, but also something you store away for future use. When you need it, it is there for you. You may choose to employ the advice or keep it for later, but either way, it is always valuable.

But without good advice, making decisions are problematic at best, comparable to playing the lottery or worse, Russian Roulette. *We all need valuable advice to make good decisions* and those that consistently make good decisions are also those that sought out good advice.

The Need for *Clear* Understanding

The second requirement for good decision making is that of *clear understanding*. It's how you process the facts that you witness, participate in, and draw from in order to justify your actions. Clear understanding is clean, and learned. It is always the foundation upon which you will ultimately build your life upon. Clear understanding is the evidence that adds to the reasoning upon which you base all of your conclusions. Understanding is good.

Getting advice without proper understanding can skew the results. *Understanding is the knowledge of how to employ the advice correctly.* Without the ability to understand, even the best advice could ultimately lead you astray.

The Need for *Good* News

Finally, and most importantly, is what we need to *hear* the most—*good news*. Unlike the other two, good news is not something you store up until you need it, and it is not something that you have to figure out or study. It is simply what you want to hear. Good news will make you relax and exhale when you realize that nothing is required and nothing is there for you to do or act upon. It is one of the few things in life that can never be bad, and it is almost always revealed when you need it most. That is what makes 'good news' the most special thing of all.

When making decisions, good news releases doubt and anxiety over the decision. For example, if you were trying to decide which car to buy, you would seek advice, understand the advice, but you justify how you make the decision based on the good reports—good news—you heard about a particular vehicle. You didn't have to decide if the news was good or not. It just is. *Good news always brings an ease of mind*, which builds upon your need for a good decision.

It was good news to us when we realized what the Perfect Plan was to become . . . it was nothing to fret over and nothing to decide upon. It is simply good, very good, news.

Simply put, good decision making is valuable advice, clear understanding, and good news. They may take different forms and point us in different directions, but all are the core ingredients of a good decision making process.

In researching and testing our insights, we learned that these three were essential to have in order with the core ingredients that were to come.

The Critical Thinking Process

Advertising has become an iconic part of American culture, and the folks who control the industry have known about critical thinking from the beginning. With the advent of radio, TV and now the internet, it is possible to "sell" your goods to anyone with the ability to hear you message. Advertising executives have known for years that the consumer is quick to make decisions on certain products, and not so fast on others. The challenge comes as consumers drift from the process and are caught in a war of push-and-pull distractions and the noise that is artificially created by some of the folks on Madison

Avenue who might not want you to think too deeply about the critical thinking process. In other words, if everything seems to be 'good,' then why bother with the proof? Well, that's how you distort and distract not how you serve, and certainly not part of the Perfect Plan.

The science that is necessary to process and understand the difference between valuable advice, clear understanding, and good news is based on a formula that all doctoral students learn on their first day of 'Critical Thinking' class. It is the 'proof' process required to convert a hypothesis into something more tangible and meaningful. It is a process that is inherent in everyone's being. The good news here is that science has a formula and it is the foundation used to prove every hypothesis and ultimately, every human decision.

The process and formula necessary to prove every *hypothesis* is this:

Evidence + Reasoning = Conclusion

The formula then slightly translates for the *decision* making process to this:

Facts + Emotion = A Decision

Let's dig deeper. Evidence is really the 'facts.' Before you believe something to be true enough to feel compelled to act on it, you must first understand the facts at hand. Science refers to this as evidence.

Once you fully understand the facts (evidence), then you combine it with what your previous experiences (reasoning) has taught you. This can be a combination of real life experiences and emotions that lead you to believe, without testing the facts, that something is true.

27

When the facts and the reasoning combine, the 'good understanding' should, if properly done, become 'good news.'

Let's look at an example. If someone makes a statement that needs to be proven in order for someone else to decide what action to take, a good scientist will apply a 'trial' test to prove whether or not the point (hypothesis) is true. Follow my logic.

Take the following hypothesis or idea: If I smash my hand with a hammer, it will hurt.

Sounds simple enough, and virtually 100% of the people reading this will agree with the hypothesis, but that's not good enough for science or the critical mind. It must first be proven.

So, how do we prove it? By creating a 'trial' that 'argues' the facts (evidence) before it applies the reasoning (emotions). The words "trial" and "argue" are important here because it implies logic. Just like a "test run" before a race, or a "test trial" before new drug is released to the public, it's the process toward the proof. The same for arguments, it is the presentation of the proof. We tend to associate the word "argue" with conflict or even a violent disagreement, but its really not. It is simply the presentation of facts leading to a conclusion. This is why you don't "present" your case to the US Supreme Court, you "argue" before them.

Once the evidence has been tested and the trial is complete, accurate, and true, the 'news' will change. It transforms from the 'advice' to an 'understanding' of certainty of the results to a conclusion which is almost always 'good news.' Watch:

1. Advice—"Better not hit your hand with that hammer!"

2. <u>Understanding</u>—"You know, hitting my hand with that hammer will hurt like the dickens!"

3. <u>Good news</u>—"Whew! Sure glad I decided not to hit myself with that hammer!"

So exactly what was the trial in this case? Well, we placed a rather dense volunteer's hand on a table and hit it with a hammer at least 10 times. After each strike, we record what happened, the results being the facts or 'evidence.' In this case, it's a safe bet to say our volunteer experienced extreme pain every time the hammer hit his hand. Therefore, the facts or 'evidence' show that smashing your hand with a hammer is painful. Sounds silly and simple enough, but that's just the first step.

Now that we understand the facts or 'evidence,' we need to combine it with the reasoning or 'emotion.' To do so is easy. We ask ourselves if there are any past circumstances that would cause us to believe that hitting our hands with a hammer will be painful. Again, we will have a 100% affirmative response. Most people, especially our poor test subject, will tell you that they have hit themselves in the hand with a hammer at some point in their lives, or at least witnessed someone doing so. So, their 'reasoning' concludes that a repetition of the trial would only result in more pain.

This creates an emotional response that overrides the particulars of any specific memory, wanting only to avoid repeating a negative action or repeating a positive experience. Either way, your gut feelings and reactions based on your past experience will be added to the facts you know, dictating your response.

So, let's look at what happens after the trial. If this sounds a lot like the legal process, it should—both are based on logic.

Evidence + Reasoning = Conclusion

1. Evidence (facts): The hand was smashed 10 times by a hammer and 100% of the responses reported that the action produced pain.
2. Reasoning (emotional response): 100% of the emotional recall and response leans toward the belief that it will, in fact, hurt if your hand is smashed with a hammer. This is based on actual and similar past experiences.
3. Conclusion (decision): Based on the facts and the reasoning, the conclusion is that hitting your hand with a hammer is painful. Therefore, I won't do it!

Facts + Emotion = A Decision

The conclusion drives the deciding action. The decision is formed from Valuable Advise, Clear Understanding, and Good News. In the case of the hammer . . . just don't do it!

Is this just simple science that seems silly? Not so. There is another part to the question that the elite 1% of the sales and marketing people know.

The question now shifts from the *process* of critical thinking to asking how much each *part* of the process weighs on the other. Better yet, does the evidence and reasoning share an equal role or does one carry more power than the other when a decision has to be made?

In science, they should be equal, but in human behavior, they are not.

Therefore, in order to better understand the decision process of a prospect or client, you need to understand how each is weighted in the mind of the decision maker—the consumer or the person you want to nudge your way.

Behind the Numbers

Science has begun to look inward for the first time ever and question theories and established 'facts' with variables that are hard to measure. Interestingly enough, we have only now become brave enough to ask humanity's only impossible question to answer: *What exactly do you not know?*

Think about it. It should stump you.

It is impossible to know what is unknown to you. If you knew it, it wouldn't be unknown. However, for what we do know, we can begin to look inward and beyond sterile logic. If science teaches us that a conclusion and a good decision is based on evidence and reasoning, then logic dictates equal order and weighting between the two. This is good in a vacuum of space, but as Mr. Spock told Captain Kirk, "Humans are highly illogical."

So, if the weighting of evidence and reasoning is not 50/50, then what is it?

We did a tremendous amount of research and looked into things we never considered when we originally drafted the hypothesis for the Perfect Plan, but in the end, we discovered the true weighting.

We now know that the average person, when making a decision, does in fact process their conclusion based on evidence and reasoning, but in their minds, it translates into something slightly different. This little tweak helps us understand the weighting of each variable in the decision makers mind, and the seemingly illogical stance that appeared to us at first. We, as humans don't necessarily process 'Evidence + Reasoning.' We actually simplify it to this:

Facts + Emotion = A Decision

So, what is the weighting between the two? It might surprise you.

The percentage of a decision that is based on emotion is around 85%. *But!* We 'justify' the emotional decision with the 15% of the known facts.

Wow! Think about that. Every decision we make is the result of facts and emotion, but we weight it with 85% emotion and 15% facts. The intriguing part is not the obvious heftier emotional weight, but the 'justification' use of the facts. We use facts to justify emotion, not the other way around. So, if we are emotionally drawn to something and want to engage, that's fine, but we need to justify the emotional decision before *acting* on the decision. Therefore, we need to focus on the justification part of the process. What does it mean to the decision maker?

The study of the world's elite 1% in nudging, encouraging, and predicting human behavior took us down paths we never dreamed of taking. One such trail took us through the logic sector of emotions. While emotions by nature appear to be far from logical, we learned that this was not in actuality true. As we dug deeper, we found, within the justification part of the process, another piece of the equation that brought sense to the Perfect Plan's Promises that we never would have seen if not for the steps necessary in critical thinking.

As we 'justify' an action that is stimulated by emotion, we found that there was a distinct correlation between the act of justification and the amount of the facts actually retained by the decision maker. As we chased the path to understanding and ultimately to the good news, we found another scientific truth: The average person only retains 6% of a presentation 10 minutes after it is done! To look at it from another angle, when you make a presentation to a person or a committee, that person can only recall 6% of your work 10 minutes after you finished. Wow, bizarre but true.

A fun little test is to watch a movie with someone from start to finish with no distractions. Enjoy and relax as if it was a routine night out. When the movie is done, wait for at least 10 minutes before asking a few questions. Make it go something like this:

"I really did enjoy the movie with you. It was one for the ages, and I am sure they have a shot at the Academy Award this year. I loved the plot and the writing was spectacular . . . oh, by the way, what was the name of the main character? How about any of the other characters? Do you remember the name of the city where it took place?"

The results may shock you. Unless they consciously set out to memorize the facts and assuming it wasn't a Spiderman movie set in NYC, they will only recall about 6% of the details. You may be very capable of describing the plot, action and even the moral of the story, but in the end, the 'facts' will leave you. This is where the other part falls into place.

We also learned that even though you can only recall 6% of the facts, you remember 100% of how you felt during the experience. This emotional retention, in essence, became the next piece of the puzzle.

Here is what we know. People make decisions based on the sum of facts and emotions. The emotions make up 85% of the decision, and they are justified with 15% of the facts. Then, within 10 minutes after the decision, a person can only recall 6% of those facts, yet they recall 100% of how they felt when they experienced the facts.

So what are they teaching us and what do the Top 1% sales and marketing teams already know? It is all about how you *feel* when you use the product or make the decision. More importantly, it has to be *real* to them. Just because the average person only recalls 6% of what you say, that does not mean that the 'facts' can be faked. It is just the opposite. What the best of the best marketing teams know is the truth behind the number. It has to do with the presenter, not the buyer.

The decision maker or buyer needs to know the truth, but more so, they need to know that you, as the expert, are truthful. You see, the fact that the perspective buyer only retains 6% of the presented facts is not a weakness, but a strength as long as the buyer understands that you—the presenter—are a truthful expert. In turn, they do not have to know what you know . . . they simply trust your expertise so they can move on with their lives and past the decision.

As it turns out, the buyer is merely testing the presenter to determine that they know the product better than anyone else. If they feel that you do, and they can feel good about their decision, you win! This only happens if they know enough to feel good about your knowledge of the rest . . . get it? It is a test.

Good Feelings about You + Facts = Justification
Justification + Emotion = A Decision

The bottom line, as Ken Robbins the founder and CEO of Response Mine Interactive, a world leader in internet Customer Acquisition and Digital Services explains, that it *"is all about trusting you with their success."* People, especially buying committees for companies, are actually looking to feel good about their decision (85%) but they need to justify it with the facts (15%). In the end, they only need to retain 6% of the facts, because they feel good about *you*. It is *you* that they are trusting and *you* who they want to engage with to make the product or service a success.

What they are telling you is that they, as the buyer, have a 100% positive emotional recall about you as a person. That's enough to move ahead. They literally trust you with their success for the decision they just made. Be careful, you have to sincerely deliver and believe in your business and your product, or it will show through and they will never believe you or trust you.

In the end, they want to trust you, but need to know that you trust yourself. That's a feeling that will carry them and you into the next stage of your relationship. The truth is, the buyer does not want to know about your product as much as they want to know and feel 100% confident that you do. You are the expert, and it is with you they trust their success.

Chapter 4

Getting a Good Decision Lesson #1

Answer the Person, Not the Question

It is really that simple. To give someone valuable advice or clear understanding, *you need to answer the person, not the question.* In other words, the question asked often reveals more about the asker than any other response they may give.

It is a core concept that was shared and executed by everyone that fell into the Top 1% category. It does take a bit to digest, because it *turns a 'reaction' into an 'action.'* The concept has a similar effect on our thinking as that of a gun being fired before you pull the trigger or an explosion before you push the detonator. It literally turns the science of our brain upside down and restates the way anyone addresses a relatively simple concept.

We are trained from childhood to sit up straight, keep our feet forward, and eat what is served. We are also taught to be polite, respectful, and answer questions clearly. While this still holds true, this key lesson revealed itself to us wedged somewhere in between these elementary social skills and the science of human behavior. It seemed more like a strategy than a response. No one on our team could get it at first, but when we sat back, unwound our brains, and were willing to accept that it is okay to add a step to the process, it all began to change for us.

To grasp it fully, you need to do what we struggled to do. Think differently about something as mundane as answering a question. When you do, you create a stepping stone to the Perfect Plan and begin to expand your unfair advantage over other sales and marketing teams.

The best in the world can tell more about you from the questions you ask than anything else you do. Knowing this, they add a step into their responses by answering the 'person' and not the 'question.' They know that the most important part of their answer is dependent on 'who' the person asking the question really is, rather than the exact answer to a specific question. Oddly, the thing that makes this difficult for most people to grasp is they think that this is nothing more than an attempt to misconstrue the truth.

This is not so. In fact, we discovered that it is the purest way to get to the truth. Dayton Molendorp, the CEO of OneAmerica Financial Partners said it best:

"When someone shows you who they really are, believe them!"

When a person asks a question, in most cases, they are showing you who they really are and the elite 1% know to believe them, and to answer the question appropriately for the person revealed.

This concept is not a means to sidestep or replace the truth, it is just the opposite. It creates the ability to answer the question with the truth that matters most to the person asking the question. The question may not, in itself, represent the real *reason behind* that of the asker. You have to be able to see past the question and look at the person asking it. This step is a strategic application of the truth—the truth that the asker really wants to hear and know so that she feels she has been given either valuable advice, clear understanding, or good news. To do this, the one answering the question has to be able to see past the question itself to what the question *says* about the asker. How does he ask the question? Why would she ask the question? What reason exists to cause him to raise that point? Knowing what drove the question will give you the insights into what *good* thing the asker is seeking.

For example, when the best of best enter a boardroom or an environment where they are presenting themselves for any type of approval or award, they immediately know how a person will respond to their answers, regardless of the question. This is done because they understand as much if not more about the person asking the question than the question itself.

The first step in doing so is to know 'who' the person asking the question really is and why they would ask the question. In other words, what is it about the people in the room that drives the question? The answer lies in knowing 'who' it is that asked the question, and sometimes it is as simple as knowing what they do in the company and how they present themselves before they ask the question.

Several years ago, my team was preparing for a presentation worth millions of dollars to our firm. We had followed the usual processes and prepared ourselves as thoroughly as possible. We knew our product, our prospect, and even their Board better than they knew themselves. Our research spanned the globe and filled over 1,000 pages of research. We were ready, but everything changed when we got there.

We drove to the prospects corporate offices the morning of the presentation prepared to present to a committee of 7 well educated and highly publicized people. They were experts in the business and were the 'dream team' of their industry. We felt prepared for this presentation and were excited to have the opportunity to present our product to these elite individuals. Soon after our arrival at their offices, we were sent into a side room to wait. Shortly thereafter, we learned of a change that took us completely by surprise.

The committee had decided to forego our part of the agenda and had delegated the decision process to another individual. The assistant conveyed their regrets and apologies . . . but that is just how the corporate world works sometimes. I thanked her and began the process of trying to reschedule the meeting with this new individual when the assistant dropped the real bombshell on us. "There is a bit of good luck," she said. "The man in charge now has arranged a bit of his time to meet with you in 5 minutes."

We had 5 minutes to prepare a presentation for someone we knew nothing about and had no knowledge of who he was or what he did for the organization. The odds of success for most would begin to immediately plummet, but we regrouped and relied on the simplicity of this first lesson. We would listen to 'who' he was more than the questions he asked.

The best of the best had already taught us the 'unfair advantage,' so now we just had to apply it. We were successful. We listened carefully to his questions to understand why he would ask them. We quickly figured out where he was coming from, so we were able to answer his questions according to what he really wanted to know. We landed the deal.

The lesson here is based on the idea that a person's decision making process is determined by his social maturity and where he was within 'the corporate food chain.' This in itself is nothing new, but to hear and see it in action puts it into perspective, thus opening your eyes to the tactics of some of the best marketing people in the world. It also gives you an inside view of the world of advertising and 'nudging' that has made up marketing plans for generations. This time, however, the nudging is done with truth and integrity above the product itself.

There are 3 classic groups of corporate buyers, and whoever recognizes these can answer the questions that are asked in a way that allows the decision maker the best opportunity to process the truth. When you know *why* they asked the question to begin with, you can give them the answer that will most make sense to them.

Let's take a look at these groups.

Group #1—The Foundation: The American Public or Why Wal-Mart, Cosco, and Target Own the World

The core of America purchasers are the wonderful workers who make up the largest buying population in the country today. They are good people who work hard but end up living paycheck to paycheck. They love their families, celebrate the 4th of July, and watch Monday Night Football. They buy American, love good music, and happen to make up 80% of the most powerful nation in the world. They are the spirit that drives America forward and makes it great. It is to these people the world owes a tremendous gratitude. They supply the world with time, talent, and treasure, but there is something interesting about the real American . . .

They are, to their own chagrin, a very predictable group.

Politicians know it, the media knows it, and marketers know it. If you don't believe it, then you need to pay better attention to the opening of sequence of Monday Night Football. You will never see a suit and tie or a corporate 'jarhead' for 100 miles in any direction. This is real America, just like NASCAR and Country Music . . . it is real.

So, how does this group make decisions? If you know the answer, you can build a model to support their needs. Economics 101 teaches you that where there is demand, you must create the supply. With this group of folks, you have to listen to how they ask the question, and it always comes back to the same answer: Price.

Yep, price.

It is the only answer they look at, and the best of the best know it. Just ask the late Sam Walton, the founder of the titanic Wal-Mart. He knew it too.

The bottom line for this group of consumers is that almost every question about every decision comes down to price. Oh, *quality* of the product does weigh some in their minds as does *where* it was made, but in the end, it is all about *price*. The Top 1% know this, and they know it is about as solid and unarguable as certain laws of physics such as gravity and inertia. To the average American buyer, it is simply all about price—can I afford this? You may argue with it, but your profound arguments still won't change the way it is.

Returning to the story above where our large presentation had been sidetracked, we only had 5 minutes to regroup and call a new play. So we focused on the basics. I got my team together and made an audible at the line of scrimmage. The play was easy to call: whoever the person seemed to be, and whatever we were able to surmise within the first 15 seconds of meeting the new decision maker, would dictate our focus.

It worked.

That morning, we met a person that became a friend of mine to this very day. No . . . more than just a friend, a *dear* friend. I had never seen him before, but the time we spent together would be the beginning of a wonderful relationship that, thankfully, has lasted for over a decade so far.

When Fritz first walked into the room, I knew we would be friends, and I also knew where he stood in life. He was—and is to this day—a worker that fell into this first group. He is a great and proud man who works every day for his family. He loves America and looks forward to the weekends and takes every vacation day with breathless anticipation. He is, for lack of any other words, real and down to earth.

I knew we would become friends, but I certainly did not know that morning that we would become such *good* friends in the years to come. My success at establishing a relationship with him came down to a quick understand of 'who' he was. I was therefore able to utilize the lessons I had learned.

Knowing that Fritz fit the perfect profile of this core group of purchasers who make the world turn and our country great, I knew he would base every business decision on one thing alone—price.

So, as we began to talk, I demonstrated respect and appreciations for his position and was able to focus on his most important variable. We lightly discussed a few objectives, just to cover a few bases, but in the end, I knew exactly who he was and what motivated him, so we gave him what he wanted . . . respect and the best price.

We won the deal without ever discussing a media board, 3 year alpha, or even a per diem. We didn't have to. By simply knowing 'who' he was, we understood where he was coming from with each and every question. From there, we were able to give him the truth he sought, even if his questions seemed to pinball about the room.

They made a great decision that day, and we are still serving them over 12 years later. By utilizing Lesson #1, we were able to get to the heart of the issues. By knowing Fritz, we knew what he was asking even if the questions seemed to ebb and flow. We became friends and business partners because we helped him. The way we helped him was to realize early on who he was in the pyramid of corporate buyers, and we respected him for that. We knew not to jump paradigms, and more importantly, we knew the golden rule of sales:

Impress your client, not yourself.

We knew why we were there. We respected him, and we never tried to impress him with how much we knew about something that he didn't. By building on the information we discussed in the last chapter, we knew that Fritz would only remember 6% of what we said, but he would easily recall 100% of how he felt about us when we said it. So, we wanted to make sure that the 6% he did recall was the most important information he needed to make the decision and feel good about it. We knew "who" Fritz 'was' and where he existed in the pyramid, and we didn't argue with it. Because of this, we were all rewarded. Best of all, the win went beyond the perceivable sale and enriched our lives even a decade down the road.

Group #2—The Middle Managers

Some of the largest institutional business models are built on the predictability of this Group, and to this day, it is shocking how few realize its power.

As we work through the social groups of purchasers within the US and place them into a vacuum of corporate America, the Foundation group, as already stated, is the working, blue-blooded American. Looking at the next floor up, we come to the upper middle class. These are the folks who tend to be a little better educated—not necessarily smarter, just more educated—have a bit more of a 'white collar' career and who, after all is said and done, manage other people in order to get things done. They are the Middle Managers.

What we learned about this group was simple, yet very, very profound. If you are in the 'game' of marketing, understanding this Group is essential. The Middle Managers always make their decisions based on *perception*.

Yep. **Perception**.

Perception is the most important thing in a Middle Manager's life, career, and thus the basis of their decision making process. Perception is a simple concept, and if you have learned Lesson #1 well, you know how to answer their questions too, because you know where they are coming from.

The Middles, as we came to call them, are never concerned with 'price.'

In their world, they are less concerned about how they perceive themselves than they are about how *others* perceive them and their decisions. In other words, it is not about how they think about themselves, but about what others think about them.

Ah, so here is the key question: who are the *others*?

Are the 'others' their bosses or the ones they manage—those average Americans discussed in the section before? Do they make righteous decisions that are good for the company and those around them even if it means risk to themselves? Or are they worried up or down the corporate food chain? Are they most concerned about the way their employees see them? Or is it all about keeping up with the 'Jones?'

The answer may not surprise you at all. In truth, the answer is 'yes' to both the food chain and what others think about them. They almost never think about the valor of selfless ambition to change the world. In the end, their decisions are based solely on how the outcome will make them look, both up and down the corporate food chain. Sadly, this applies to corporate decisions, as well as personal decisions.

So, who are they trying to impress?

The Middles do worry about perception, and it goes both ways. They have a keen sense of awareness of the ebb and flow of management as it goes both up and down . . . or shall we say *through* them. In their world, they are fixated on making sure those below them in the corporate food chain 'perceive' their decisions as managerial, thus maintaining their integrity and credibility with those they manage. They are also concerned with making sure that those above them (the 'Cs'—CEO, CFO, CIO etc . . .) believe and perceive them as worthy for promotion so that one day they can become a 'C' as well.

The Middle Managers in the world are incredibly predictable because all they care about, regardless of the question or intent, is perception. They make strategic decisions based on their understanding of what is necessary to maintain their 'boss' perception to the working class while also trying to make the upper echelon believe that they deserve to be one of them.

The Top 1% know this principle and accept it to be true. They are able to understand and, in some ways, sympathize with the Middle Managers. This became a fundamental truth when we realized that the Top 1% are able to see through the smokescreen of the question and understand what they are really asking is, "How does this make me look?"

The Lesson also relies on the understanding that Middle Managers don't always realize why they make the decisions they do. Thus, the presenter can wade through the irrelevant issues and get down to what is most important to the client. The best of the best know that perception is only combated with another 'law' of physics: matter cannot be created or destroyed, just reshaped or reformed. Translated into more mundane terms of marketing, perception is always the motivation for a decision and is always present, but it often takes the form of a *brand*.

Brands mean more than anything.

Brands are perceptions.

Brands translate into quality, low risk decisions that no one complains about. Just ask Fidelity Investments.

Fidelity runs one of the best families of mutual funds in the world and has, without question, some of the best and brightest people in the world working for them. For more than 4 decades, Fidelity has taken care of Americans'—and the world's—retirement plans, investments, and trusts. They are really, really good. They are also really smart and totally understand Group #2—The Middles.

The proof is in the pudding. For years, Fidelity has been the dominate player on Wall Street when it comes to managing large

Fortune 500 type company retirement plans. They are brilliant and deserve every client they have, because not only do they do a wonderful job for their clients, they also understand what others don't . . . the decision to award large corporate retirement plans is not made by the C's (CEO, CFO, CIO, etc . . .). The decision is made by a committee of Middle Managers and signed off by the C's. So, since the Middles only make decisions based on perception—both up and down—and the word 'perception' is best translated to 'brand,' Fidelity built an empire by building a *brand*.

Once they had established themselves as a global brand, they had it won. They knew that when a committee of Middle Managers met to decide on contracts and to whom they would award the biggest opportunities, Fidelity was a sure fire winner. They had the quality, low risk, and recognizable brand. They made the marketing 'hat trick.'

Fortunately, Fidelity never wavered from a commitment of excellence, and they were able to take their brand and superior work into a market that was looking for something stable and trustworthy—something that would not destroy careers or credibility. Fidelity now does trillions of dollars of business with America's best companies because they understood Group #2. Middle Managers make decisions on *perception* and perception really means *brands*. Fidelity also understood the lesson mentioned earlier in that people, by making a decision, trust you with that decision's success. Fidelity delivered.

My favorite example of understanding the 'middles' comes from someone who most people would agree is one of the 5 smartest marketing minds of the past 100 years, George Zimmer, the founder and Executive Chairman of Men's Wearhouse, Inc.

George began with a single store, a hand painted wooden sign, and a cigar box as a cash register. Today, it is a publically traded company with over $1 billion in annual sales. George was always driven to serve the customer and fill his needs, but he also knew who his customer was and why they bought from him. While Men's Wearhouse did provide everyday low pricing, George brought credibility to his primary customer by creating and reinforcing the greatest advertising tag line of the 20th century. George knew that the Middles were all about perception, so he said it best and closed all of his commercials with a simple statement, "You are going to like the way you look—I guarantee it!"

To this day, it is one of the best examples and executions to understand why the Top 1% are different. Like George Zimmer, they know 'who' and 'why.'

No one, up or down, ever questions a solid brand, and therefore the 'perception' the Middle Manager craves is accomplished. The Middle Managers appear smart to the foundation working class and reliable to the upper class. Perception is created, saved, and a decision is executed.

Group #3—The Cs (CEO, CFO, CIO, etc . . .)

What does your landscaper have in common with Wall Street's CEOs? Good question. Let's find out. As we studied and worked our way up the corporate and social ladder of decision makers, the field became narrower as we reached the apex: the C's.

The C's are a unique and dynamic group of ladies and gentlemen. They are usually hard workers who sacrifice a lot in their lives to make it to the top. They are bright, well educated, sometimes smarter, and usually deserve the position the have obtained.

The C's make their decisions differently than the first two Groups do. The Top 1% of the world's sales and marketing teams understand this because, in many ways, they evolved through the same social and corporate system along a similar path—although there is a difference in attainability that we will discuss later.

It quickly came to our attention that the C's, while they may seem mysterious and untouchable, are actually the easiest to understand. The decision making process was the same for this group no matter if they had to wade through the mud and muck of social and corporate climbing, were born to it, or simply developed the maturity to attain it. Either way, the C's based their decision on one thing alone: Return on Investment.

Yep, Return on Investment (ROI).

It sounds cold until we unlocked the secret known by the Top 1%.

What we came to discover is that the pinnacle of social and corporate structures actually make their decisions in a similar manner as Group #1 (the blue collar workers) does with a slight twist. Instead of *price,* the core concept to reach the C's is in one word: *investment.*

The Top 1% implemented everything they knew when dealing with the C's. The basic principle and key concept of answering the *person* and not the *question* still reigned true. They still wanted to give and get good advice, understanding, and news. For the best of the best, the 'who' in this case is always simple to determine, so before answering their questions, the Top 1% asked one of their own to the C's, "What exactly is your investment?"

We were shocked at the answer!

100% of the time the Cs answered the question in the way the Top 1% knew they would. Investment is *not* a monetary term or an accounting issue to the C's. To them, the word 'investment' meant 'time.' Literally, clock time . . . tick, tock, tick, tock.

The C's all wanted to know what the return is on the *time* spent and allocated to the deal, not the dollars. In other words, "Is this the best use of our talents, assets, and dollars for this allotment of time? And what do we get in return?"

Wow! We were shocked. Ironically, we had heard this concept before, and you would never guess from where.

In the northern suburbs of Atlanta, it seemed that on some days every other truck and car was a landscape vehicle. These are the guys who make the world look better by transforming our yards and corporate centers into freshly cut and groomed portraits of beauty. They have redefined our expectations of the way things should look and the image we portray. Simply put, this is a beautiful place to live.

The landscapers are the guys you miss and respect the most if you ever travel overseas, especially to Eastern Europe and Mexico where they don't have these services. You can also get a keen sense of how far we have come here in America once you look at any family pictures from the 1960s or before. If you do, don't look at the Disney trips or resort visits. Focus on photos of family gatherings and kids playing in parks. Look at the great outdoors of the time. There were little to no flowers, and the lawns for most Americans were mixed seeds and rarely had the 'carpet' appearance we have grown accustom to viewing today. While we might take them for granted, they have added a creative touch to America that helps us *feel* as great as we are. The landscapers keep the place green and clean when no one seems to notice, or really give them the credit they deserve . . . everyone that is, except the C's.

30 years ago, America was a different place. If anyone told you that TVs would be flat, we would pay for water in bottles, or that 5th graders would have cell phones, you would have laughed them off the street. Better yet, if you were told that almost every home would be paying for someone other than the 13 year old boy down the street to cut their grass, you would be equally humored. But it has happened.

What caused such an evolution that it has come to define our interpretation of success? Did anyone, other than the Top 1% ever ask why? Not really, but the truth was there, and it was the same truth that the C's understood about their decision making process and most importantly about the idea of *time*.

As the market and demand for landscapers grew to such large proportions, it became obvious to the insiders that it was never about cutting grass, but all about 'buying back' valuable time. While it is true that most people enjoy the work and actually might want to cut their grass, the time that it takes versus the cost that the landscapers charged is the best return on your investment in the world. If you don't believe me, ask yourself a question. If you cut your own yard, how much time per week do you spend to make it look its best? 2 hours? 3 or 4 hours?

Ok, reverse the question. How long would it take a landscaper to do an equal or better job for you? 45 minutes? 1 hour?

Next, unless you are retired, find landscaping your primary form of exercise or therapy, how much does the 4 or 5 hours you spend on taking care of your own yard mean to you? Can you use that 4 or 5 hours for something else? Can that time be better spent with your family or working on something more productive and even income related?

If the answer is 'yes,' then how much would you spend to 'buy back' those 4 or 5 hours and what could you make once you have the time back? You see, time really is money and a deployment of resources. So you need to know *how* the 'time' is being spent.

The C's—corporate officers, business owners, and those who have reached a certain level of maturity—make decisions based on the allocation of resources necessary to make the best and most desired return. The most valuable of these resources has not changed in a thousand years. It is time itself.

The Top 1% have grown accustomed to this and understand the process better than anyone. They know not to approach the C's with a low cost offer, because *price is for the masses*. They also know that *'brand' carries little weight with the C's*, because they aren't interested in what others think about them. They just want *to understand performance as it relates to the allocation of time* and resources.

In some ways, the decision making process of the C's is the easiest to understand. It is about quality and the impact it has on their mission, not what others think or how cheap it is. The Top 1% know this and respect them by giving them a different approach to the offer. The Top 1% serve and help the C's grow and accomplish their mission, regardless of price or brand. It is about the best quality for the maximum performance for the time spent on the project.

In the end, one of the most profound things we learned from the Top teams was to understand the reason why people make the buying decisions they do. The first step in the process is to know 'who' that person was and, if they are a corporate buyer, where they fit in the corporate hierarchy. *If you know 'who,' then you know 'why.'* That is the foundation of enlightenment that takes you on the path toward the Perfect Plan.

Before we get to the Perfect Plan, there are a few more Lessons to learn.

Chapter 5

Getting a Good Decision Lesson #2

Who is in Charge?

The second lesson we learned leading up to the Perfect Plan seemed to fly in the face of traditional sales and marketing training, but by now, we were expecting these lessons to defy accepted practices.

For centuries, sales trainers have firmly placed in the minds of their students that they, the sales and marketing professional, must take control of the process to make the sale. They are taught that they are the captain of the ship and they must lead the prospect to the land of milk and honey. In order to sell—or so they are taught—you must take charge and never forget the ABC's of sales: Always Be Closing. The sales person is king and must drive the prospect to the decision they need in order to buy the product.

You guessed it . . . this is wrong!

The Top 1% know this entire concept to be false and so chose to fly in a different direction than that of classical training and management. They do so by asking another simple question, "Who is in charge of the meeting?"

The answer is somewhat surprising.

The person in charge of a meeting—any meeting—is the person who is being judged by the outcome of the decision. Please repeat this in your mind and even reread it—it is one of the critical factors leading up to the Perfect Plan:

The Person in charge is the person being judged by the outcome of the decision.

So, how do you know who that is? The process is rather simple as long as you don't underestimate anyone in the room. For the best example, let's go back and finish the story I started in the beginning of the book.

$450,000,000.00 is a lot of money, remember? It is a story I have used to painstakingly illustrate the power of the Perfect Plan and the unfair advantage it gave us. As today, we dominated our field, and with such a significant win, we felt we were on top of the world.

Except for one person . . . and that person was *not* the CEO.

As you may recall in the earlier rendition of the story, after we had finished our presentation and executed perfectly all 3 lessons of getting a good decision by using the Perfect Plan, the CEO came all the way around the boardroom table to congratulate us on our win that day. She noted our professionalism and told us that she felt sorry for the other 2 teams who were still scheduled to present after us. She even went so far as to ask that we return the following Monday to begin work and even offered a celebration dinner for us the following night. It was simply the best feeling in the world . . . a $450 million win!

Later that night, I met the broker who had referred the business to us for our standard celebration cocktail that I call, "Daddy's Lit'le

Helper." I looked up, saw my friend and longtime colleague, and instantly knew something was wrong.

I have been in the 'people and marketing business' for a long time. I have grown accustomed to the polite smiles and obligatory handshakes. I had also come to know when someone was masking his or her emotions or just going through the motions. In this case, there was no façade. He had bad news, and it was written all over his face.

He sat down, and I knew he had been given one of the hardest jobs in the world. He had to not only tell me that we did not win the business, but that they had reversed the original decision to award it our way. That's a double whammy for sure.

I had known him for so long and our friendship was too close for anything to become personal. I knew it and so did he, and that actually made it worse. I know he wanted to tell me that they simply didn't like us or we lost it due to rudeness. He would be thrilled to just walk away and chalk it up to someone else being better, but that was not the case. He had to tell us about a mistake we had made, and he knew that would hurt worse.

We have a saying in our office, *"99% of academics can be beaten by 1% of politics any day."* We knew this, so we strived hard to cover both sides of this pendulum, but while we can't control the politics, we can the academics. We consider the Perfect Plan to fall on the academic side of the pendulum. We had worked too hard and rehearsed it too many times for it to come down to a sloppy mistake, so I was hoping it was politics . . . it was not.

My buddy got straight to the point, and I appreciated that. He was as shocked as I was, but in the end, he was in the best place of all. Brokers are responsible for bringing in 2 or 3 choices to the client, and we, while favored, were just one of the choices. So, he wins either way, and part of his greatness is that he never puts a client in a position to make a bad decision, so any 1 of the 3 would be fine for the client. But in this case, even though the CEO awarded us the business, she apparently reversed it and went another direction.

"Why?" I asked. I wanted to know if it was something we said or if the others had outflanked us and simply did a better job. If someone actually beats us because they are better prepared and deserve it, I cheer for them, but if we lose on our own merits, I don't find it a very happy outcome.

"You would not have believed it," he said. After the CEO awarded us the business, he had walked us 45 feet out of the boardroom and to the elevator, congratulating us on our victory, but by the time he returned, the room had changed directions.

"I was amazed at how quickly they turned," my friend told me. "By the time I was back in the room, they had reversed their decision and wanted to see the other options."

"Why?" I asked.

"Well, it was the IT guy," he informed me. "He actually said the most dreaded words in the world, and the Committee responded to it."

By the way, this committee, with the exception of the CEO who was there as a courtesy to us and our past history together, was made up exclusively of 'middles.' The entire committee was made up of their middle managers!

I was astonished. "What could he have possibly said to reverse a CEO's decision and influence over a group of middle managers?"

My friend soberly quoted the IT Manager, who said "'if we go ahead with this, we will be judged poorly by the outcome of this decision.'"

He did it. He killed the deal. He reversed their decision.

The IT Guy, after not saying a single word during the entire presentation spoke the most dangerous words he could ever say to anyone, especially to middle managers. As a result, he became the most powerful person in the room and the person in charge.

So for a quick review of Lesson 1, we learned that *middle managers make decisions on the 'perception' they think others have about them.* And we also learned that *the most powerful person in the room is the one being judged by the outcome of the decision.* So, it all came down to one statement. The middle manager IT executive, who was concerned about how others would perceive him, preyed upon those truths regarding the other 'middles' in the room, sending a resounding message that they received quite readily. They turned and ran from the idea of "we will be judged poorly by the outcome of this decision." A double whammy to the gut.

While I knew the decision was made and committees rarely reversed a direction once set upon, I had to ask what it was that made the IT manager think the way he did and why he had felt compelled to share it with the committee.

"It was simple," my friend explained. "Your web site was not to his liking, and he felt his employees and peers would judge him poorly if they went in that direction."

"You have to be kidding me!" I blurted out. "For $450 million, I will build him whatever website he wants!"

"I know," my friend told me. "But the seed was planted and they moved on."

So here is where it really hurts. I asked him who they decided to go with and how did they address the web issue. I had overlooked it, never thinking it to be a factor (my mistake for sure). "Well, the team they chose never showed a website. They just mentioned that they could build whatever he wanted."

So there it was . . . proof again that validated one of the things we had learned in the study and trials of the Perfect Plan. The 'Middles' only care about how they are perceived to others, and the person in charge was the person who was being judged by the outcome of the decision. In this case, the manner in which the IT manager delivered his fear to the committee was so broad based that the rest just filled in their own mental blanks and reversed the decision. The CEO was in a terrible position. If she over ruled the committee, she was in actuality telling them they were all wrong, but since she herself was one of the Top 1%, she knew better than to try. These Lessons are like laws of physics. You might not fully agree with the result, but don't argue with them . . . you will lose.

What did we learn?

Well, with a 95% close rate from the Perfect Plan principles, we knew this was part of the 5%. However, in an odd way, we were excited. This loss only helped fortify in our minds that the Perfect Plan was the secret to the world's best, and we—regardless of how good we were—are just as subject to the lessons and principles as anyone else. We overlooked someone and underestimated him. The client was a large University and we had focused on their education business, when in reality, all schools are becoming IT driven and their future looks a lot different than the brick and mortar that makes up campuses today.

We really were excited with what we learned, because we applied another simple truth we learned along the way. After every meeting—win or lose—we ask two questions of our own team:

1. What did we do right today?
2. What could we do better next time?

The Top 1% had taught us that you never ask what you did *wrong* or all you do is second guess yourself. If you are the best, you already believe that you did everything possible . . . given the time and talent you had at the time to be your best. If you fall short, that's okay, but celebrate what you did right and learn what you can do better next time. We did, and our close rate soon grew to 98%!

I had the pleasure of seeing David Feherty interview the great golfer Greg Norman once. Clearly, Greg Norman is a stand out in the world of the Top 1% with 91 career victories, a ranking as the number 1 golfer in the world for 331 weeks, and countless business success stories from his clothing lines, vineyards, and equipment sales. It was a great interview, but what stood out to me the most was when David asked him what drove him towards his success. His answer was not about gaining fame and fortune, but simply about his unquenchable desire to know that he always did his best. Anything short of *his* best was not acceptable. It had nothing to do with a win or a loss. He noted that if you gave your best, and someone else wins, that's fine. Give them the credit they deserve, congratulate them and move on, because you gave it your best. However, anything short of your best is a problem. That is what made him so great. He went out every day (and still does as of this writing) with the intent on being the best he could be. This focus is one of the key components we found among the Top 1% we studied as well.

The next day, when we were all back in Atlanta and had gotten back into the routine, we did our post game review and discussed the two questions. We knew we had done our best and that's what we needed to know in order to go forward, but next time, we would be better and never ever underestimate anyone else again. We got better and that is a fundamental trait of the Top 1%. Always, always, always, get better.

Chapter 6

Getting a Good Decision Lesson #3

Bringing It All Together Before the Plan

As we have learned so far, the Perfect Plan is based on a few fundamental 'absolutes' that help prepare you for the Plan itself. We know that all anyone really wants is an 'unfair advantage.' We learned that Valuable Advice, leads to Clear Understanding, and then to Good News.

Facts + Emotion = A Decision

We discovered that people make their decisions based on 85% emotion, but justify it with 15% of the facts. We know that after a presentation, the average person only recalls 6% of what you said, but 100% of how they felt about you when you presented it.

Good Feelings about You + Facts = Justification
Justification + Emotion = A Decision

We now know that if you know 'who' someone is, you know 'why' they make the buying decisions they do. And then we learned the most important lesson of all: the person in charge is the person being judged by the outcome of the decision.

Okay then. Let's bring it all together.

The Top 1% of the world's sales and marketing teams follow a distinctive plan that sets the decision maker into a position of making the choice for them. The Perfect Plan is the sequence of events that forms a presentation style that makes these teams of people stand out above all others, but it's founded on the fundamental truths listed above. These truths are scientifically proven and, until fundamentally shaken from their perch, need to be treated as if they were physical laws of nature. You might not agree or understand them, but they are nevertheless true. If you respect them, as the Top 1% do, you can build on a formula that almost guarantees success.

Before every presentation and meeting, the best individuals and teams spend hours building their case even before they employ the Perfect Plan. In order to do so, each of the fundamentals listed above are vetted and displayed in order to avoid any mistakes or miscues. 'War Rooms' are built and designed so that these functions can be graphed, charted, and displayed. Multiple views are taken and talent levels grow for everyone, but the simplest thing of all is the most important to know.

Asking Who and Why?

If the presentation is business to business, involving committees or key executives, then it is vital to know who they are, and the best place to start is in cyberspace.

The onset of Facebook, LinkedIn and the Social Media Culture has opened new doors to help the Top 1% know as much as possible about the decision maker before they ever meet. Some folks might find it creepy, but others relish the ability to draw focus on the presentation and to drill down to a level where there are no distractions or hang ups. The web and social connection is merely a saving grace of time and talent. In the past, presentations were blinded without any understanding of 'who' the decision maker really was. Outside of a few country club connections or downright cloak and dagger spying, there was little to know. In as little time as a decade, technology, social, and business interactions have advanced enough so that the presenter can use these tools not to twist and distract, but to neutralize any distractions.

Social Media makes life better and helps us present in the most honest way possible. Prior to the Social Media explosion, sales people were classically trained to lump everyone into a handful of categories and taught to motivate people via a technique called "Disturb and Motivate." These presentations were usually canned or scripted for a broad based audience, sales and marketing at the face-to-face level drifted into a dark void that preyed on people's emotions. The challenge was simple. Before the science was explored and truly understood, the belief that buyers were emotionally driven to make decisions already existed. While we know it to be true today, we also know how the process is weighted.

Remember, decisions are based on 85% emotion and justified with 15% of the facts from which you only remember 6%, but you recall 100% of how you felt.

In the past, these numbers did not exist, so all of the weighting was placed on emotion and how you felt, but it was misguided by the belief that you should expose the negatives of a client's current situation and show them their 'pain' in order to motivate them to change. Looking back, it is amazing anything was ever accomplished in sales and marketing, but as cultures adapt, people became accepting of or immune to any particular phenomena so that it either grows or dies. In this case, the 'pain' technique seems to be fading to a slow death, and that's a good thing.

For a very, very long time, the Top 1% have avoided these 'disturb' or 'pain' techniques, because they always knew that the client is looking to them to know the business. That's why clients only remember 6% of what is said, because they don't *need* to remember as long as they know the presenter knows what he is doing. As stated before, they are trusting you with their success, but you have to earn it. It has to be real, genuine, and sincere. No faking it.

The Top 1% also know that even though their clients recall only 6% of the data, they remember 100% of how they felt about the presentation. So think about it. If the foundations leading up to the Perfect Plan are true, and the prospects recall 100% of how they felt when they were with you, then why in the world would anyone want to create an environment based on fear and pain? In other words, the 'disturb and motivate' guys did a great job of making the client uncomfortable with their situation—which was, ironically, their goal. Yet when or if the client did decide to change, they decided to do it with someone other than the presenter. They went a different direction, with someone else. Why? Because all they remember about the presenters is how they felt—bad! On their way to successfully creating pain and disturbing their prospect, they also created an association of that pain to themselves. It became Pavlonian.

Ivan Pavlov was a Russian psychiatrist who founded the 'reflex conditioning' theory. He believed that people responded by reflex to certain conditions. His study became famous for experiments such as ringing a dinner bell before feeding his dogs. After some time, the dogs would slobber from just hearing the bell ring as the sound brought instant anticipation of food.

Ivan went on to prove (evidence and reasoning) that certain conditions can stimulate a response purely on a learned reflex. Well guess what? He was right, but western sales and marketing over the past 40 years has misinterpreted its use in the art of influencing human behavior. The only thing that came of it was the classical sales training of the 1960's through the late 1980's (some still linger today) which utilized these 'negative' techniques. They may have motivated the change, but the individual in question often reflexively went with someone else in their efforts to change because there was no 'pain' associated with that other person.

I had a unique inside track of an effort to prove that the 'disturb and motivate' techniques do not work. For years, I have had the pleasure of serving at the Summit Counseling Center (Atlanta, Georgia) as Chairman and President of their Board. Summit is a fantastic organization that delivers over 7,000 clinical hours per year in counseling to help people through rough times and out of dark places. Their services included everything from relationship counseling, career, addiction, abuse, suicide and grief counseling. All in all, Summit is a magical place of healing.

With the leverage that my position provided, we decided to incorporate the academic strength of some of the best and brightest counselors and doctors. I actually went straight to the top and presented the theory to lead director of Summit, David Smith. What we decided to do, in order to prove the 'disturb and motivate' techniques would fail while the Top 1% succeeded by simply avoiding what the others manufactured on purpose, was to create a list of emotions, both good and bad. We would list the good emotions on the left and their opposites (bad) across from them. Once we could visualize them, we were able to track and study their use in a scientific manner that revealed their counter balance.

As we began to list emotions, we found that there were more emotions than anyone could reasonably track. I spent some time trying to reverse engineer the emotions we felt after hearing a presentation from the Top 1%, but that quickly became much harder than I thought it would be. That's when I realized that the list was right under our noses. I had just finished a fantastic book by Alan Hunt, PhD. Alan is an old friend and a wonderful guy who happens to have a doctor's degree from Yale in First Century and New Testament studies. His book, *The Fruit-Full Living*, focused on a first century bad guy that turned good, named Saul—better known as the Apostle Paul. In one of Paul's many letters from that time, most of which make up the New Testament, he actually laid our list out in perfect sequence. When Paul was communicating back and forth to his many churches, he actually listed the emotions and character he felt they should try to achieve, knowing that even the most negative and harmful individuals could not argue with these essential feelings. Once I realized how perfectly suited this list was to the study, we listed them as such:

1. Love
2. Joy
3. Peace
4. Patience
5. Kindness
6. Goodness
7. Faithfulness
8. Self Control

The brilliance behind Paul's list is that, 2,000 years before the first 'Behavioral Economist' came into existence, he actually created an emotional structure that allows one emotion to lead right to the next in such a way that virtually 100% of psychiatrists today agree with the progression. For example, once you have love, you then find peace. Once you have peace, you find patience, and with patience you find kindness, and so on. They perfectly build upon each other, and we found the list perfect for our study.

So, then we had the best doctors and counselors discuss and list the opposites of these emotions, and frankly, the results shocked us. I thought the opposite of Love was Hate, but it's actually *Fear*. The opposite of Self Control is Hopelessness . . . just ask any addict.

The list is given below:

Good Emotions	Bad Emotions
Love	Fear
Joy	Loneliness
Peace	Anxiety
Patience	Uncertainty
Kindness	Lack of Respect
Goodness	Envy
Faithfulness	Lost
Self-Control	Hopelessness

From here, we began to watch and observe. It was quickly and overwhelmingly apparent what was happening. Once we had a barometer—the list above—we were able to watch when certain sales and marketing individuals and teams who were not in the Top 1% jumped into the right side of the chart and began the 'disturb and motivate' process. It became so obvious that you could actually see the build up and even the attack coming as these folks purposely created an environment driven and fueled by bad emotions.

They went out of their way to find a reason to support the need to inflict fear, loneliness, anxiety, and hopelessness on the people they were presenting to. It was amazing for us to watch people's faces adopt a negative look on purpose—as if anything good could come from it. We tracked their success rate and even followed up with several of their clients to test the impression they had made, and it was indeed as we suspected.

Actually, the close ratios of the sales teams who created bad feelings were higher than we expected, around 8%. As you can guess, however, the follow up with the clients followed an unsurprising theme. Several of the clients were motivated to make a change, but close to 100% of those who did not engage these 'disturb and motivate' teams cited a 'bad feeling' when recalling the presentation or the team. Many went on to say that they had enough 'crises' in their day to day business activities that they had no desire to invite someone in that seemed to make them feel distracted and demotivated. More than one went on to explain that the 'disturb and motivate' team eventually made him feel stupid for making what he felt at the time was a right decision. So, not only did he second guess his decision, he felt even worse about himself. So, why would he ever want to invite that feeling or the person back? He would not, and he never did.

As you can guess, the Top 1% were the exact opposite. We watched in amazement as they stayed on the 'good' side of the emotional fence the entire time. Even when the realities of a challenge would surface, they brought it back to the 'good side,' regardless of how bad the challenge may have been. The science was once again backed up as we determined their close ratio to be 95%. Indeed, the exit interviews with the prospects were overwhelmingly focused on the good feelings they had about the team and their message. They felt confident that the Top 1% team were experts and could deliver. All of them were magnetized to the team's good nature and positive aspect. They even, on several occasions, gave us unsolicited compliments, listing the positive emotions they felt from the Top 1% teams.

From here, the Top 1% teams were able to create a situation that was best for everyone, a position founded on research and based on the foundational beliefs that it is not 'why' but 'who.' When they knew everyone in the room, and what the probability of their decision making would be based upon, they would overlay several of their charts to create the most likely scenario. The key to all this work and preparation is founded on a desire to neutralize any distractions. This is done so that the prospect or decision maker was focused on the positive truth, and not a random negative act, that would distract and capture their attention on the wrong thing. Not unlike the situation I observed in New Orleans 25 years before, the Top 1% didn't want to be judged by how they parked their cars. *In the end, they just clear the slate in order to deliver a clear and effective presentation.* They earned the right to be the best, and the services they provided exceeded all expectations.

The Top 1% know that before anything can be presented, a foundation must be laid. From that platform, they can build a reason for the client to know that they can be trusted with something as precious as the prospect's own success.

This is the point where it all begins and where Plans are executed . . . Perfect Plans.

Chapter 7

The Promises of the Prefect Plan

As we discussed in the brief of Chapter 2, The Perfect Plan is the organized process and outline followed by the world's Top 1% of sales teams and marketing professionals. It is the proven combination of sincere work that is based on a foundation that neutralizes any distractions so that complete focus can be attained on the presentation. From there, something magical happens.

The Perfect Plan is a series of 3 Promises and 3 Beliefs that collide in a presentation so the prospective buyer or decision maker can positively answer 3 simple questions in their own mind. Then and only then can the engagement begin and the purest relationships emerge.

Let's examine each of the Promises and see how they eventually collide with the Beliefs to create the magic.

Promise #1—Gratification, an Attitude of Gratitude

When you become aware of the process and the patterns of the Perfect Plan, the first of these Promises quickly becomes apparent. Any competitor will agree that the most critical move of any game is always the first one. Traditionally, it is where one of the parties involved tries to command the high ground and thus gain a classical advantage. Not so with the Top 1%. Their first step is seemingly in the opposite direction. It is one of humble and sincere *gratitude* and heartfelt thankfulness demonstrated towards the client. The first step is to genuinely reverse the field and give the prospect the high ground by letting them know that you are grateful, appreciative, and thankful for their time, effort, work, and even their very existence. In its purest form, it is the beginning of a relationship based on an 'Attitude of Gratitude.'

Anyone who has ever seen the Academy Awards presentation, *The Oscars*, knows that the acceptance speeches all start with "I would like to thank . . . ." This is where the award winner begins to list all of the people who 'helped them get here tonight,' and 'who made it all possible.'

We have all heard these lines before, and for most of the audience, it is the point where we get to see "who" the Actors really are and where their appreciation is founded. Most of the speeches are genuine and sincere with a humble gratitude and a few tears of joy. Occasionally, we do get into one where a little sleep sets in because some actors can't rescue themselves from a verbal flop by yelling, "Cut!" While it might mean something to the Actors who are reading from their lists—and even a little to those to whom the names belong—it really does nothing for the audience. We decided to ask "Why?" Why does it work for some and not for others?

For some, the names they read are in thankful cadence, but never seem to make it past the viewer's ear canal. It is just chatter to the millions who are at home and watching it all unfold. But why is that? What is it about those movie star persona's that turns your brain away? It's simple. There is a disconnection between you and the seemingly insincere words that have nothing whatsoever to do with you. While the Oscars seem to magnetize you to the show itself, there are a few whose lack of personal connection drives your conscience away. Without the ability to bond, there is no appreciation for the words. The best know better, and those special moments, even as distant as they are both physically and personally, become something special.

Genuine, sincere, and heartfelt *Gratitude*, on the other hand, is something uniquely different altogether. Though not exclusively our own discovery, the best of the best found that *Gratification is the greatest emotion to bond two people together*—or any relationship for that matter—more than any other single event, emotion, or activity.

A recent study from major southern university confirmed what we already knew was true. They had a hypothesis, and they asked a very simple question to test it. They asked married couples who have been together for over 60 years about the key to their longevity in matrimony. They wanted to know what kept them together for so long. Is there one thing that they did different than anyone else? The answer was a resounding 'yes.' They did do something different. They built their relationship on an Attitude of Gratitude. Each said, in almost unanimous fashion, that they felt their spouse had a deep and sincere appreciation for them. They were genuinely thankful for each other and, as a result, have been able to *bond* for over 60 years!

So, of all the emotions possible, the one that bonds two people—or organizations—together, more than any other, is the grace of gratitude. The 'Attitude of Gratitude' creates a bond that builds and builds with no end in sight. It becomes a connection that glues people together indefinitely.

We were able to prove what the Top 1% already knew and had established. A bonding occurs when there is an obvious and sincere thankfulness expressed for a person's presence and very being. We watched as the best already knew this and had incorporated the concept into every presentation and every meeting they walked into. Everything they do starts with an Attitude of Gratitude or what I like to refer to as a 'Face of Grace.' It is an attitude that becomes magnetic, compelling the recipient to bond with you on unconscious levels.

The first action is not to attack or take the high ground. The first act is one of humble grace that sincerely bonds them to the prospect. They do it with an act of gratitude.

Promise #2—Clear Education

After you establishing a bond through appreciation and gratitude, you begin educating. Education is a little bit different within the Perfect Plan than what you may think or have been exposed to in the outside world. So many people approach me during a Relationship Training Course and ask, "What do we say? What do we talk about?"

I often respond, "I have no idea, but pick something and let's talk about it."

True as that is, there is a key to increased success that we learned from the Top 1%. Their magic was founded on the premise that they never pick more than 3 things to talk about. You see, the Top 1% know that humans of any race typically only remember 3 things from any given conversation or presentation. Americans who speak English are a perfect example. Adult Americans have a short attention span—about 20 minutes max—but that also limits the number of things they can focus on at any one time. So pick 3 things that you need to educate your audience on and lightly, ever so lightly, cover those 3 things. The goal here isn't to impress them with facts, figures, and reams of data. It is about building trust.

Here's the truth. The people you are talking to, the very people you are trying to convince, those you are trying to take action, don't care what those 3 things are. And they don't really want to know. What they want to know is if you are trustworthy.

Can you be trusted? Can they trust you?

If they so, then they can trust what you say and what you *haven't* said.

Today's business to business environment lives in a state of constant crisis. *Most businesses are either in a crisis, leaving a crisis, or running to a crisis . . .* they certainly don't need more crises in their lives. So, what they really want to do is trust you with their success once they believe they have the good news that you are the expert and can trust you. What they clearly never want to do is become the expert themselves. People just want to know that you are the expert and they will recall enough to justify that you are who you say you are, even if you have not said that much.

This is provable.

As you now know, a decision is the product of Evidence plus Reasoning—or Facts plus Emotion. This is important to understand. People may only remember 6% of the 3 things that you say, but they will remember everything they *feel* while they are with you. They *will recall 100% of how you made them feel after they forgot most of what you said.* How many times have you returned home from an activity, can't recall everything that was done, but certainly recalled how you felt?

"Boy, I really had a good time!" Most of the facts you will forget, but the feeling is what you remember forever.

Interestingly enough, we found that every time you use a number in your presentation you risk losing half your audience. This applies to domestic US sales as well as international sales. People rarely follow a train of numbers in a presentation, and when presented with a multitude of numeric facts, begin to mentally check out of the process. When this is combined and over seeded with the actual topics you are educating the prospect with, it can become a deadly combination. During our study, we found that 3 topics were the perfect number for success, but when pushed beyond three, the law of diminishing returns became evident. Whenever a person receives 3 topics to digest, it sets the base line for success, but when a 4th topic is added, the probability drops by 25%. When a 5th is added, it drops by 50%, and a 6th topic actually creates a total crash with a return rate close to 0%. So what does it tell you?

Go back to basics. *The prospect is not looking to be educated in the classical sense.* What they what is to be educated on the 'good news'. It is the validation that you know the material so they don't have to. *They are literally listening in order to 'justify' their decision.* As we discussed, decisions are the sum of evidence and reasoning or simply put, facts and emotion. The decision is based on 85% emotion but justified with 15% of the facts. Additionally, 10 minutes after your audience leaves the room, they will only recall about 6% of everything you said, but they remember 100% of how they felt when you said it.

So there you go . . . they don't want to know as much as you think they do, so maximize the probability and respect their roles in the process. Pick three things and stick to it.

The Top 1% know this very well. When they pick 3 things to talk about, they chose the ones that create an emotion of trust. They may leave trying to remember what you said, but they know that they totally trust you—that you will deliver—you are the expert.

You need to explain what they need to know, but only the amount they are expecting. Ultimately, it is about creating trust. "I don't need to know everything, as long as you do; I'm good with that and I trust you." This is the attitude you are trying to build.

The 'Education' step in the Perfect Plan is the biggest challenge most people face. Too many times, we end up backwards in our thinking. For more than 25 years, I have worked with brilliantly smart sales and marketing people, and it is common to see them stumble and make simple mistakes in this area.

So many people commit the cardinal sin of *education*. They are more interested with impressing themselves than their client. This is when we usually see the 'show up and throw up' maneuver. It occurs when a sales person feels compelled to tell the prospect everything he or she knows, even if it takes all day and covers a hundred relevant or irrelevant topics. It is usually the key ingredient to any failure. It is difficult, even for the most well trained professionals, to restrain themselves, and that is what makes this step so hard.

Your job is to win their trust by making the complex seem simple, without taking away from the integrity of the subject matter.

Ultimately, that is all the client really wants and longs to hear.

Steve Jobs said it best when he referred to how difficult it is to take difficult subject matter and simplify it for the consumer. In a Business Week interview in 1998, he said, *"That's been one of my mantras—focus and simplicity. Simple can be harder than complex: You have to work hard to get your thinking clean to make it simple. But it's worth it in the end, because once you get there, you can move mountains."*

The Top 1% begin each presentation with an Attitude of Gratitude that builds a bond. Then they build on an environment that creates an emotion of understanding. In other words, it is the "I get it!" moment. Remember a time in your life when the light bulb flipped on and you said those words? Do you recall what it was you *got*? Perhaps you can, but I bet your remember 100% of how you *felt* when you got it.

Education is about justification and the good news that comes with it.

Promise #3—Ease of Business

The 3rd Promise and the final step in the presentation sequence that the Top 1% follow is to make it easy for the client. We call this *Ease of Business*. In our research, we determined that the best of the best followed these three Promises in the exact *order* given here to create the Perfect Plan. You must start with the Attitude of Gratitude and then move to a clear Education, before making it simple and *Easy* for them to get on board.

People are busy and already feel their lives are complicated. Most people and businesses live from one challenge to another. As we learned in the Education Promise, they are either headed towards a crisis, in the middle of one, or just leaving one. Either way, they don't need your crisis, and they will balk if that is what they see you offering them.

What they need is someone that is going to make their life a little bit easier. If what you offer makes it easy, simple, and crisis free, they will engage in it. This generates an emotion of relief, like a vast burden has been lifted from their shoulders. You want them to think, "Wow, when I am with this person, it is so easy!"

Once again, the Top 1% create the emotion of gratification. They start with the bonding emotion of gratitude, the facts of justifying and educating, and then close with the emotion of relief.

Have you ever had someone step in and just solve a problem that you figured would never get solved? Have you ever had a deadline that you didn't think you could meet when someone stepped in and made it easy? Remember the feelings? Immediately, either consciously or subconsciously, you felt like you could work with this person and, indeed, wanted to work with them. The relief someone feels by knowing their life is easier because of you is overwhelming to some.

Ken Robbins, the CEO of Response Mine Interactive in Atlanta, often talks about the transition from the sale to the application as being the most critical step of any business. People are so used to being sold something that never seems to do as advertised that they prepare for the worse. In today's business to business world, the translation of this feeling might build an emotional response associated with regret or anxiety of the future association.

The Top 1% know this to be the most critical step, so they create the opposite effect. After bonding with gratitude, clearly educating them with trust, they swing all their focus into relieving the prospect of any worry from that point forward. It has to be easy. After the prospect has 'justified' it in the education step, they need to feel relief, knowing that with the trust given comes ease of business. It has to be delivered and executed with care, knowing that this, in the end, is what they want the most.

Ease of business is what makes it all worthwhile.

Summary of the Promises and the Importance of Their Order

We actually went back and experimented several times with the order presented here by the world's best. We did everything possible to see if there was another way. We went back to the Top 1% and presented alternative orders of presentation and across the board, they dismissed it. They weren't even willing to try to do it differently. They knew it was in a specific order for a reason, and they could easily predict the results of taking them out of sequence.

1. Attitude of Gratitude
2. Real Education
3. Ease of business

It has to be in that order with no negotiation.

By now, we had grown to believe in these folks and knew that whatever they told us was true, but in the end, science has a passion of its own, and proof needed to be obtained through the familiar path of evidence and reasoning. So, since the Top 1% were not willing to try, we decided to run the test with those who were considered 'great' marketers, though not in the world's Top 1%. It was here that we were struck by a revelation so far outside the box that it almost made everything too simplistic, nearly setting us back in our search for proof. As we began to test and retest on the second tier sales and marketing teams, a story from my past came back to me and finally made sense in and of its self.

Several years before, when my life was simpler in a BC (Before Children) era, I set a goal of winning my golf club's coveted 'most improved player' award of the year. I committed to the work as well as the time, training, and lessons necessary to improve my game. So, after studying the path to success and squaring in on my commitment, I went to our club pro and announced with great pride my intentions. That's when he told me the undeniable truth. I remember his words like it was yesterday. Clear, concise, and cogent, he never hesitated to embrace my emotion when he simply said, "It will never happen, kid."

"What!" I exclaimed. "You obviously don't know how hard I am willing to work."

He was gracious as he pulled up my handicap and began to explain. "I see you are an 18 handicap," he said. "That's solid and in line with the rest of the world."

"Yeah, but I want to get that down to a 7 or 8—maybe even a 5."

"That's awesome and certainly a great goal that I know you'll achieve. I have seen you on the range, and I feel we can get you there with some commitment and little hard work."

With the abrupt switch to praise, I was a bit confused. "Shouldn't that get me the most improved award? Who could possibly move farther up the ranks than an 18 who gets to a 5?"

"Well," he said, smiling, "that's not exactly how it works. You see, with hard work you can certainly hit your goals, but doing so doesn't make you the most improved player. That belongs to an elite group, and you just are not there yet."

My curiosity picked my bruised ego up off the floor and stuffed it safely in a pocket somewhere in my heart. This was interesting and I bent an ear to understand.

The pro continued, "The most improved is not the 18 who gets to a 5, but the 2 that gets to a 1 or even a 1 handicap who gets to a scratch. It's in the elite circles that improvement becomes truly difficult, not in the novice ranks. It is so much harder for an elite player to improve by a single stroke than it is for a club player to practice a bit and shave down his handicap with a few successful rounds. That shouldn't take you away from your goals, and in a few years when you get closer to that elite status, you'll understand. Simply put, the better you are, the harder it gets to improve."

It sounded right, but I must admit that I would not realize how truthful he was until we began to study the best of the best, and even reached that status ourselves.

This is why the Top 1% didn't want to change up the order. They knew it worked, and to them it was fundamental, untouchable. So why mess with something that wasn't broken? Once we knew their commitment to success and understood the handicap system of golf and life, we had no problem experimenting with the top 20% who were willing to try. We had to move outside the Top 1%, because they knew better and wanted to leave it alone. You just don't mess with science, even if you have to prove it to yourself.

When we did experiment with the order, we decided to focus on the traditional apex of those considered top achievers by their respected fields, but still not quite in the Elite 1% range. We looked at the bell curve of corporate America, to use those in the Top 20%, and who were willing to try to do things differently. They, the top 20%, were encouraged to participate in an event out of order from the Perfect Plan, and were asked to build on relationships differently than those in the 1% tier. The group was wonderful and eager (a lot like me with the golf lessons) and they allowed us to document and tweak the experiment as we shifted the order and asked for their assistance. It was grand and we were thrilled, but in the end, just as we expected, it was a disaster . . . .

Fortunately, what we learned and were able to ultimately prove with facts and emotion was that *the Perfect Plan absolutely has to be presented in the proper order: Gratification, Education, and Ease of Business.* Bonding through the emotion of gratitude, explaining the facts simply, and then bonding with the emotion of relief, is how the Top 1% *always* do it.

It's almost like a sandwich or hamburger. You sandwich the facts between the emotions, knowing that they will most likely forget most of the details surrounding the facts, but trust that *you* know them . . . and that's good enough for them. If they know you are grateful, they in turn will be thankful that they are with you and that you have made it easy. Then, and only then, will they respond, "I'm going to do it!"

Attitude of Gratitude = Emotion and Bonding → 100% Recall
Real Education = Facts → 6% Recall for themselves but Trust that you are the expert
Ease of Business = Emotion of Relief → 100% Recall

You see, it's not enough to *sell* someone. People knowingly or unknowingly prefer to be with people who share a common belief system. They want to work with people who they feel they *know* and *trust*.

The order of the Perfect Plan's three promises is pure in the most logical way. It establishes the bond, delivers the facts, and relieves the person by an easier way of doing business. *The order is Perfect* in itself, but there is more to it. Today, I can create a TV commercial using Attitude of Gratitude, Real Education, and Ease of Business, and it would get some significant results on the marketing trackers and rating agencies, but that is not enough.

The missing element is the human connection, the bonding that builds trust and the feeling, "I want to be around this person." Watching a TV commercial doesn't answer the question of 'who' you are or 'what' you believe. Knowing what you believe is essential to the process of trust. People always want to be with, and do business with, those that they feel are on the same page. That's what drives us into the next silo of the Perfect Plan: the Beliefs.

People will bond and emotionally justify the reason why they should take action, but the Top 1% have another unfair advantage that only begins once their 3 Promises collide with their 3 Beliefs.

Chapter 8

The Beliefs of the Perfect Plan

The Beliefs of the Perfect Plan are just as important as the Promises, and when the two collide, you will have given the prospect everything he or she needs to answer the following questions:

1. Is this right for me personally?
2. Is this right for me professionally?
3. Is this right for me spiritually (in my conscience)?

Once a person can emphatically answer, "Yes!" to all three of these questions, he will choose to agree with whatever it is you are presenting. Remember, a person will always recall how he or she felt when with you, so your Beliefs must shine forth.

It goes without saying that when it comes to belief systems, everyone and every culture is unique. There are a *lot* of different systems that propel people forward in life. Some are based on hard work, others focus on forward thought, but seldom does anyone stop and ask the question, "Who are you?"

One of the amazing facts found in the Perfect Plan is centered on the actual *individual*. The Promises are unique and can be taught, but there is another variable that brings it all together and it is based on 'who' the Top 1% really are as a *people*. They are groups who, like many others, have a belief system that varies from person to person and culture to culture.

In our research, we found at least 20 different beliefs that made up the 'who' of the Top 1%, but there were 3 that existed in all of them. Regardless of where they were in the world, 100% have them in common. These 3 Beliefs were so prominent that once we realized their existence, it became obvious that they were the key that made these folks so great.

The "Ah-ha!" moment came one day when we realized that the same formula used on the Promise side of the equation existed in equal proportion with their Beliefs. Just as the Promises worked in an order that bonded with emotion, followed by the facts, and sealed with emotion, so did the Beliefs. The emotion/facts/emotion grid reigned true with the Beliefs! In fact, they carried the same logic and profound wisdom. The Promises were a statement of what the Top 1% *did* for the prospect, and the Beliefs were a revelation of *who* the Top 1% were as people from the heart.

These 3 beliefs make up the collision point between the Promises of the Perfect Plan and the understanding of 'who' you are.

Belief #1—Create, Don't Compete

Everyone would agree that there is something special about a creative person. You would also agree that after painting a room or doing anything artistic, a person feels a profound sense of accomplishment that feels unlike any other emotion. The emotion created when someone is in the act of being creative, or just the observance of someone else's creativity is staggering.

When we studied the vast variety of emotions that a person might feel or express on any given day, we noticed a parallel between the bonding of Gratitude and the stimulation of positive emotion. As we dug deeper, we found an equal energy that is emitted by the 'stimulation' felt from the emotion of Creativity. This is in complete agreement with the studies conducted about couples bonding for 60 or more years via Gratification.

We once believed that Creativity was in and of itself only an isolated act or a physical motion—an action—but we quickly discovered that Creativity is an *emotion* as well. It fell into the same category as Gratitude. A person can easily express Gratitude by works and deeds, but the receipt of Gratitude is 100% emotion. The same is true for Creativity. It can be an action, but to be *part of* the actual Creativity requires the act to morph into an emotion. It is a very special transformation. We discovered that much like Gratification, Creativity is a magnetizing emotion based on stimulation. *When someone senses another's Creativity, they become magnetized by it and stimulated to be with or around them.* The Top 1% know this.

The other side of the coin is that most sales and marketing folk focus on the wrong action. Instead of *creating*, they focus on *competing*, and this is wrong in the eyes of the best, who believe that their job with the client is to create, not compete.

Competition is a big word in a variety of different ways, and if you study it, it is possible to get lost in its origins and meaning. Its English roots translate to 'an act striving for supremacy between static performers.' Thus, if you are competing, you are the same as your opponent, static, or average. In a way, today's culture seems to embrace competition, but for all the wrong reasons. One of the sidebar studies we completed within the Perfect Plan centered on the concept that true competition would result in an equal distribution of win/losses. What was it that broke the mold for the Top 1% who reigned supreme in their fields? In our quest for an answer, we studied sports that spread their season out over several months and played the most games. Within the US, it came down to Major League Baseball and professional basketball (the NBA). What we discovered was fascinating.

At an elite level like the NBA or MLB, talent was the key to getting teams into the postseason playoffs, but it was the *coaches* that actually won the championships! If you look back at the greatest coaches of all time, most had multiple championship wins with different teams and talent: Joe Torre (Atlanta Braves, New York Yankees, LA Dodgers), Tony LaRoosa (Oakland A's, St Louis Cardinals), Phil Jackson (Chicago Bulls, LA Lakers), John Wooden (Indiana State, UCLA—10 Championships in 12 years with different players!). The list goes on and on.

So why do coaches win championships and players don't? It's all about creativity.

Coaches have the ability to make 'chess moves' within a game, to creatively use the talent and tools available. He can call timeouts, substitute players, call plays, and much more. They execute team work with their leadership and use their Creativity to see beyond the field of play. Like the Top 1%, the 'talent' of their product and team was superb, but it was—and is—their Creativity that defines them. No one can deny that the market place is full of others trying to bump you off your perch, trying to win the same client, but the belief system of the Top 1% allows them to forgo thoughts of competition. They never want to be the same as the rest. They are different and they magnetize people to them with their Creativity, not by competitive flair.

They weren't there to compete for the client's business at all—they never thought about competition—they never wanted to be anywhere near such a concept. Competition was never part of the equation.

I like to talk about this when we do our Deep Dive training sessions. The word 'competition' comes from Greek, Latin, and old English root words which mean 'static' or 'the same.' So think about this . . . when someone says, "I am competitive" or "I am competing," they are saying that they are "the same as everyone else".

We found this to be a universal belief. People want to be around those who are creative and innovative. *People are attracted to those who, in their very body, soul, and spirit, are creative.* The Top 1% established their Creativity immediately, faster than anyone else. They projected a complete attitude of "I am here to create. I am a creative person."

Another, not so scientific, means of proving this point is the Food Network. This is a great organization that is changing the way America looks at food, making it fun again. In a meeting, I asked how many in the audience had ever seen the Food Network on TV. About 80% of them raised their hands—the other 20% were no doubt lying. I then asked how many of them had actually attempted to make any of the food demonstrated on the network. Less than 15% indicated that they had.

Here's the point, the Food Network isn't banking its success on their viewers actually *duplicating* what their chefs make. They know that what attracts you is the fact that their chefs are *creating*. This is the magnetizing emotion—the stimulation—that they create with you.

This is why people will watch the show at 2 in the morning. There is an attraction to creation. It is part of our belief system. We like to watch people take nothing and make something of it. Think about it. The Cup Cake Wars? How can they make a successful show around *cupcakes?* It's the creation. It's the innovation.

It is creation and being creative that is important to the Top 1%, not selling a product.

Create. Don't compete.

Attitude of Gratitude (Emotion) -- Create! Don't Compete (Emotion)

Education (Facts)------------ Belief #2

Ease of Business (Emotion) -- Belief #3

Belief #2—The Value Is Greater Than the Cost

The second Belief that the Top 1% convey to a client is that the value of what they are offering is always greater than the cost of that object or service.

Once you establish a bond of trust with a client, clearly educate them, establish that this will make their lives easier, let them see that you're creative and on top of the situation, and then show them that the value of what you are offering is greater than the cost.

We mentioned earlier that every time you use a number in a presentation, you lose half of your audience. People have preconceived ideas of value. If you tell them how much it costs without sharing your belief in its greater value, you will lose those who automatically think the cost is greater than the value. Buyers are conditioned today to believe that numbers are never valid or sincere. We know from Promise 2 that American buyers can only comprehend 3 topics at a time, and most other cultures are the same. This comes from the way we sequence numbers in our mind, and with English, we are in a terrible position before we ever get out of the gate . . . The English language actually set us up for failure!

Let me give you an example. In English, we count 1 to 10 with no issue, and then, without rhyme or reason, we develop the number 11 and 12. What is strange here is that these two numbers break the total logic of the sequence in their *word form* (eleven and twelve). There is no sound that assigns a number 1 and 2 to the Ten to create the eleven and twelve—it just appears.

But never worry; the English language gets back on track with the teens. *Thirteen* is really 3 plus 10—expressed 'thir' (three) and 'teen' (Ten). Then 4 and 10 for *fourteen*, and 5 and 10 for *fifteen* and so on, all the way to 'twenty' or 2 tens. It makes perfect sense, but just to make life difficult, we flip the order. Instead of continuing on the same sequence of sounds—logically putting the one in front of the 2 tens (twenty)—we flip the sounds and say *twenty-one* or 2 tens and 1. It is the exact opposite of the sound pattern we used in the teens.

English, in the first 21 numeric sequences between the number 1 and 21 actually changes the logic of how the language sounds 4 times! No wonder people are afraid of numbers. It also contributes to why English speaking American kids seem to struggle with fractions. Then to top it off, between the illogical combinations of the language sounds, we start to break it down into 'st,' 'nd,' 'rd,' and 'th' (1st, 2nd, 3rd, and 4th) and really create a problem.

The result is clear. English speaking buyers have trouble with the numbers when they repeat or get too complex. What they really want and need is a 'trusted Advisor' or sales person to help them understand that the 'value' really is greater than the price—or put another way, "Hey, this is a good deal for me (the buyer)."

It doesn't matter if the cost is something they pay, you pay, or someone else pays. They just want to know if the value they are getting is real.

This is why it is so important that they trust you. If they trust you, then your Belief in the value of whatever you are offering will be another bond that you establish that in reality becomes the fact they decide on. Remember, in Promise 2, we learned they will only remember 6%, so all they want to know is that *you* know, that *you* are confident, and that *you* are sincere. It is the same here, if you build on the confidence and trust by simply stating your Belief that the value is greater than the cost, the next step is forward and toward a conclusion.

The value is greater than the cost.

Attitude of Gratitude (Emotion) Create! Don't Compete. (Emotion) Education (Facts) ------------ The Value is Greater Than the Cost (Facts) Ease of Business (Emotion) -- Belief #3

Belief #3—Give Forward

The third Belief we found the Top 1% possessed is something that, quite frankly, astounded us. For the first 8 years of our research, we had it worded incorrectly. Nevertheless, it is the core Belief that weaves throughout their entire belief system, no matter what they were trying to sell, do, or achieve. In the end, they never ever gave back, they only gave forward.

I'll say it again. They gave *forward*.

We originally labeled this 3rd Belief as "*giving back*", but in fact we found this to be untrue. The Top 1% didn't give back. They didn't dance around this 'tit for tat' concept of you give me something and I'll give you something in return. There was never an obligation or contract—explicit or implied. There was never any condition or expectation. They simply *gave forward*, and they did so without any expectation of anything in return. They gave, and gave again.

I mean that exactly as I wrote it. They were not concerned with getting anything back. That wasn't what was important to them. This is a unique concept to most business models and thus, all by itself, becomes a game changer. When they approach someone, they say, "Here's what we are doing for the community or for you, and here's what we do. We want you to have it." If you are uncomfortable with the idea or think it to be bragging a bit, then don't—because they give forward anyway. Most people would be shocked at how often opportunities present themselves to give, and the best always do it without question and without an alternate agenda.

The Top 1% from around the world, from any culture or any language, all shared this core Belief. They are, across the board, giving people. When someone is giving for the right reasons—and the correct reasons are essential for this Belief to work—then people pick up on it. It makes the Top 1% highly attractive and trustworthy. There is a special aura and glow about them. To give and have no intention of looking for a reward or to make a sale is unique and special in today's world, regardless of where you live and the language you speak.

Giving comes in all shapes and sizes. It can be basic and monetary in form. It can be physical, a presence that is there when needed, and it can be the use of a talent on behalf of another. One of my favorite stories of giving came from one of the Top 1% while telling me how another 1%er had made an impact on him in his early years.

Danny Strickland was a young eager college graduate who wanted to take on the world. He was the first in his family to attend and graduate from college, having grown up on, as he puts it, "the wrong side of the tracks in a town already poor and beaten down."

He was lucky, and knew it. Through a series of fortunate events, a lot of hard work, and commitment, Danny made it and graduated from an elite northern school with a chemistry degree. It was 1970 and he was instantly in demand. The space race was in full throttle and the cold war loomed in the back of everyone's mind. Danny was offered a great job with one of the nation's leading firms, Proctor & Gamble, and he jumped on it. Already aspiring to change the world, he envisioned himself working on top secret projects for the military and even, hopefully, working with astronauts and NASA's finest. Danny knew something great lay ahead for him, and this job matched his plan to make a dent in the world ahead. He knew he had made it when he was asked to step up and take over a new project for P&G as a Technical Brand Manager! Without hesitation or even asking what the job entailed, he jumped at the opportunity and committed to being the best they had to offer.

"What could it be?" he thought to himself. "Maybe something to do with fighting the Soviets or better yet, something that would take me to the White House to meet the President." The anticipation almost killed him before he ever set foot into his new office or met his new team.

The next morning, he woke up early and practically ran to P&G headquarters to receive his new assignment and his first crack at something big.

They gave him his assignment. At first, he refused to believe what he had heard. Had they really said that? Did they really want him to do *that?* Yes they did.

"Laundry detergent?" he echoed in disbelief.

After a moment of dazed incoherence and confusion, the words rang in his head like Sunday Church bells. "Laundry detergent?" he repeated, dumbfounded.

"Yes," they said. "Welcome to Big Soap."

At the time, this was a huge part of Procter & Gamble's revenue. "Big Soap" as they called it made up over 50% of their revenue, and it was something they could produce that everyone used. However, to Danny, it was more about what it was *not*. It wasn't astronauts or a spy chemical, and it would most likely not get him any invitations to the White House. What it ended up being was a *start*.

On his first day with his team (one analyst and a part time secretary), Danny had the pleasure of meeting someone, who, looking back on it, was a 1%er himself. Bob was his name, and in 1971, he was someone who saw the world in a different light than most people could imagine. Bob, without ever knowing it, was about to start a chain effect that would change the world, all by giving forward.

When he first approached Danny, it seems a bit consolatory, like a big brother comforting his younger sibling because he did not make the varsity team. But it was really one of those 'wow' moments that can change your life in a profound way. As they sat together, Bob began to share some of his wisdom with Danny that was rich in *valuable* advice, *clear* understanding, and ultimately *good* news. Bob knew that Danny was disappointed in the unforeseen turn in the road of life that now was taking him to Big Soap. What happened next, however, will change *your* life forever. Yes, you read that correctly—*your life . . . you who are reading these words.* It certainly changed Danny's life.

Bob gave Danny a charge that sounded so simple that the profundity of it resonated with Danny for the next 40 years.

Bob told Danny, "If you want to change the world and make a big impact, you have to make a decision. You must decide if you want to help people improve the quality of their lives."

"Of course I do," Danny said. "But I'm working on soap . . . laundry detergent to be exact."

Bob smiled and continued, "You see Danny, the decision you need to make is not about *if you want to impact their lives,* but *how you are going to do it.* How do you want to affect the quality of their lives?"

Perplexed, Danny listened as Bob went on to explain, "You come to a point where you have to decide. *To change the world, you will either do something big for a very few people, or something small for a large number of people.*" He paused and fixed Danny with a gentle but serious eye. "So, decide. Do you want to do a little for a lot, or a lot for a little?"

Knowing that Danny was absorbing the advice, he went on to help him understand further. He told him about an impact on the lives of people that comes with no glory or awards, but affects people beyond their own imagination. He pointed out that everyone around

Danny wore clothes that they had to clean every day. "That's the 'a lot' part," he said.

So, if everyone you see is doing something similar, and you can make a small impact in that area that affects the quality of their lives for the better, then you can change the world! Even, if it is just laundry soap.

"So," he concluded, "why don't you come up with a way to make their clothes brighter and cleaner quicker? What would it be like if you could affect their lives in the smallest way, but in turn, everyone gets a little bit ahead?"

Danny found, in Bob's giving forward of his wisdom, *valuable* advice that led to *clear* understanding, and ultimately changed the world with *good* news . . . it began with a project to take phosphates out of detergent and ended within an icon—Tide Detergent. From there, Danny went on to work on Era, Downey, Gain, Oxidol, Ivory Soap and Drift. He literally changed the world for a *lot* of people in a small way, and only a very few knew it.

A few years later, Danny got the call he had been waiting for. It was time for a new project. He felt great about what he had accomplished and was finally ready for the lime light. Then it happened again. Danny was so good at what he did that they wanted him to start a new division to make the world a better place, but guess what?

As Danny likes to say, grinning ear to ear, "What could possibly be less sexy than detergent? How about diapers . . . *adult* diapers!"

Danny almost passed out, but the drive and determination to change the world kicked in, and he took the job on with a passion. As he began to think through the market potential and see the true needs that existed out there, he thought back on Bob's wisdom and began to try and find a way to affect people's lives, even without the glory or fame. He soon learned that the number 1 reason people were entering nursing homes at the time was for incontinence (the lack of bladder control). The social stigma and lack of adequate care had created an open door for perfectly productive people to enter unproductive nursing homes—just because of the embarrassment of incontinence. That's when Danny decided he would change the world for a lot of people yet again, but in a very small way. He threw himself into his work and focused on the opportunity to help others in ways no one had before. In the end, he did it, and it changed lives.

To this day, Danny gets teary-eyed just talking about it. "You would have never believed it, but for the first time in modern history, people began to *leave* nursing homes to resume their lives and become happy and productive in society once again." He remembers receiving letters of sincere gratitude from people all around the world that he never met, but who thanked him for saving their lives.

He did it. A *little change, for a lot of people, made the world a better place* because of the wisdom someone had given him "*forward*", some 40 years before.

From there, Danny finally did realize his dreams, but he never forgot what Bob had taught him. He repeated that advice over and over in a career that made an impactful and generative leader to several of the world's largest consumer goods companies, both in the US and in Europe.

When Danny officially retired, he had made it. As the Senior Executive at Coca Cola in charge of all product, innovation, and brands, he had made a career that impacted millions of people around the world, and one that will be felt for generations to come. From juice to sports drinks, and even bottled water, Danny was there. He literally changed the world, all because one of the Top 1% gave forward with time and talent all those years ago.

As of this writing, Danny still gives forward. His foundation has funded schools and scholarships to help people that will never know who is impacting them or why, but he, as a Top 1%er himself, still remembers the words from Bob, and never ceases to give forward.

A little for a lot, or a lot for a little.

Either way, you affect the quality of people's lives, and you *give forward*.

Attitude of Gratitude (Emotion) →Create! Don't Compete. (Emotion)

Education (Facts) ------------- →The Value is Greater Than the Cost (Facts)

Ease of Business (Emotion) --→Give Forward (Emotion)

Chapter 9

Bringing it All Together

Getting in the Mind of the Decision Maker with the Perfect Plan

People need assurance before they make a decision. For many people, spending money is a fearful thing. You know that you want something in return for spending it that outweighs the actual cost of the item or service. You want value. But before you take that step of committing yourself, you will want to trust the individual. When you add Gratification, Education, and Ease of Business you have the basis for establishing trust with your client or prospect.

In the case of the world's Top 1%, *they* would begin by establishing themselves in the bond. Once the bond is established with an Attitude of Gratitude, they were clearly educated, and lives were made easier. Then, they would share their belief systems. They were there to create, not to compete. They knew that the value of what they were offering exceeded the cost and made certain to share it. They wanted to give forward without any expectation of return.

We already learned that people will remember 100% of how they felt when they were with you, but only 6% of what you said. This sets the foundation for the patterns and logic on both sides of the

Promises and the Beliefs, and it is based on the sincerity of the one presenting . . . the Top 1%.

Think about it with this simple chart:

The Promises	The Beliefs
Attitude of Gratitude *Emotion = 100% recall*	Create, Don't Compete *Emotion = 100% recall*
Education *Facts = 6% recall*	The Value is Greater Than the Cost *Facts = 6% recall*
Ease of Business *Emotion = 100% recall*	Always Give Forward *Emotion= 100% recall*

When the 3 Promises collide with the 3 Beliefs, you have a magical moment. It is something amazing to witness. When you see it, you can't help but to exclaim, "Wow!"

But here is the incredible part. This entire belief system is powered by something that every Top 1% sales and marketing person knows to be true! They know, at the moment the presentation ends, when the perfect order of Promises are supported by the perfect order of Beliefs—in a collision together—that the decision maker who just witnessed the event will make a decision based on the answers to 3 simple questions:

1. Is this right for me personally?
2. Is this right for me professionally?
3. Is this right for me spiritually (in my conscience)?

Gratitude (Emotion)----> <----Create! Don't Compete. (Emotion)

Education (Facts)----> <----The Value is Greater Than the Cost (Facts)

Ease of Business (Emotion)----> <----Give Forward (Emotion)

⇓

Is this right for me personally?

Is this right for me professionally?

Is this right for me spiritually (in my conscience)?

Every consumer, decision maker, parent, student, couple, and thinker ultimately asks these questions of themselves before they make the decision final. The best of the best know that the answers have to be an *affirmative* to all three questions, because only then can there be harmony in the decision maker's mind.

All three areas, Personal, Professional, and Conscience, must align or there is no deal. Even though some will push and pull to try and make a marginal call on one of the three, it never works for them. All three areas must be 100% in confidence and each must stand alone. Once they do, the decision is viewed as a perfect, harmonious one.

The best of the best know this, but in their elite way of thinking they answer these questions for the client in their mind before it ever begins. The Top 1%, in their own way, will give forward in an effort to make sure that the answers to these questions are 'yes!' Only when the Top 1% believe that the answer to all 3 questions is 'yes' for the client will they actually make the presentation.

This is Good News!

This is where everything began to turn upside down for our team.

This is where we began to see it clearly.

It was almost a heart stopping moment, much like watching a great mystery movie and you realize the character you thought was the bad guy, wasn't. In our case, they turned out to be the good guys, or even better, the perfect guys.

You see, this is where we came to our own conclusion, when we realized that we were wrong all along.

In an effort to discover how the Top 1% of the world's sales and marketing teams performed—trying to discover the secret—we found a revelation within The Perfect Plan. The men and women we had determined were the best sales and marketing people in the world *didn't consider themselves to be in sales and marketing!*

What? It was true enough. They didn't believe that they were sales or marketing people, nor did they ever refer to themselves as such. For all those years, the secret key to their success remained hidden from us until that very moment. We had a momentary panic when, for a fleeting second, we saw the entire project flash before our eyes. Did we miss something?

It was a strange sensation at first, but then we realized what had happened. We had *valuable* advice, we found *clear* understanding, but now . . . above all . . . we finally received our *good* news.

What we learned was their secret.

You see, the Top 1% are who they are because they don't see what they do as an opportunity to sell a product or a service.

They see it as an opportunity to *serve!*

That was it. That was the missing link!

The pattern was Perfect—we knew that much. *A series of 3 perfectly aligned Promises that formed a bond of Gratitude they would never forget, gave clear Education that created trust in the presenter's expertise, and followed by an unforgettable and relieving emotion of Ease of Business.*

These Promises were met by a Perfect Belief system of 'who' the presenter was and what he believed. They were magnetizing with creativity and they never competed. The value was greater than the price, and above all, they gave forward . . . without any expectation of anything in return.

When they were done, the prospect or decision maker would consciously and/or subconsciously ask themselves 3 questions:

1.   Is this right for me personally?
2.   Is this right for me professionally?
3.   Is this right for me spiritually (in my conscience)?

If the answer was 'yes' for all 3, then a harmony existed so that they knew the decision to be made was good and Perfect. The Top 1%, however, took it one more step further. This is where the light turned on and we understood why what they did was always *good* news.

The Top 1% never start with the Promises and Beliefs. They actually start at the end.

They do so by asking themselves ahead of time if the prospect is able to answer the 3 questions with a 'yes,' and if so, that's where they would start. Why? Because that is what servants do.

They understood something that was a world changer for us. Many have explained to me that we live in a world where most people confuse the words 'service' and 'process.' Many of those who say they are in the 'service business' (i.e. financial services, food services, and even medical services) are not in the 'service business' at all. They are in the 'processing business.'

Process people move items and people from A to B, from one place to another. They become drones, and their customers just flow through their turnstiles, looking for the next process to ride. But for those who understand the good news of the Perfect Plan, 'process' is not what they do. They are legitimate *servants*.

When we discovered this truth, it changed the dynamics of everything we had learned. It was a moment I will never forget. We discovered that *the main difference in the 'service business' and the 'process business' was not in the procedures, but in those executing the deal.* They taught us that to truly be in the 'service business,' you yourself had to be a 'servant.'

In order to 'serve,' you have to humble yourself to where you can actually *be* the 'servant.' Then and only then will the Perfect Plan make sense.

It is a 'servant' who will ask if the decision is right for those they serve personally, professionally and in their prospect's spirit.

It is a servant who serves with a bonding Attitude of Gratitude.

It is a servant who clearly educates the client that they, the presenters, are the ones who will carry the burden, not those they serve.

It is a servant who makes other lives easier.

105

Why? Because that is what a servant does.

From there, when asked, "Who are you?" a servant explains, "As a servant, I am here to create and not compete. As a servant I will always provide a value to you greater than the price. As a servant, I will always give forward."

"Why?"

"Because that is what servants do."

Servants anticipate the needs of those they serve. So if I, as your servant, know something is good for you personally, professionally, and spiritually, then I will offer it to you because it benefits you. This is the basis of *real* service.

Why? Because that is what a servant does . . . he serves.

So the Top 1% are special because they start at the end.

This is because they aren't in the sales and marketing business, and to our surprise, they never were. They are in the Servant Business. They are servants and that is the Perfect key to the success of every single sales and marketing individual in the Top 1%. They seek to make sure that what they offer is good news for the client. They want to benefit the client, serve the client . . . not sell him something.

This is why the Perfect Plan is so perfect.

Once something is right personally, professionally, and in a person's gut (spiritually or their conscious) then they will pull the trigger on a decision. The Top 1% already know the answer to these questions *before* they ever present the deal. The presentation from that point on is to make sure the client sees the truth and does not get distracted or confused with irrelevant thinking, and to present the service in a pattern that is perfectly suited for them to receive you as a servant . . . but only if it is right for them.

Those who practice the Perfect Plan always begin with the question, "How can I best serve them? From there they begin with . . . I will show them how *grateful* and *thankful* I am. I will *educate* them clearly on the subject. I will make it *easy* to work and be with me. I will also weave in *who I really am,* because they want to trust me, not a product or a service. They want to work with someone with a similar value system, so I will demonstrate how *creative* I am and show them the full *value* of what I am presenting is much more than the cost of it. Then they will know that I have already given forward on their behalf without the thought of anything in return, because I value their relationship more than the product or sale."

This is not how the traditional world of "Sales and Marketing" train people to think, but it is most certainly how 'Servants' think. Be careful now; don't confuse 'true servants' with those who tout that they are in the 'Service Business.' In actuality, the people who claim to be in the 'Service Business' are most likely in the 'Process Business.' They are just processing things from A to B. They process a sale from beginning to end. That is not *service.* Service can only be delivered by a *servant.* And a servant is someone who humbles themselves before another and says, "I am here for you." They know that relationships are more important than products and they have already determined that this is right for the client, serving the client's interests.

Do you see why this entire process just blew our minds? We were all there looking to see what the Top 1% of the sales and marketing people did only to discover that they weren't in Sales or Marketing. They were Servants. Their presentation wasn't a pitch to sell something.

It was a humbling of themselves to serve the interests of the client. This made them genuine and sincere.

Wow.

The results were off any measurable grid, and that's why no one paid attention to them. Management systems couldn't comprehend it or wrap their heads around it. They figured there had to be a trick and they couldn't figure out what it was. But it wasn't in the *what*. It is always in the *who*! *Who* they were is what made a difference.

We have had countless industry professionals, some internal to our own organizations, ask to borrow or even purchase our "materials". They do so believing that it is the proposals, books and pitch books that make the sales, but in all actuality it is the way we humble ourselves and show that we are servants. It is never the materials, but always the person.

Somebody asked me once, "You really love what you do, don't you?"

I enthusiastically answered, "Yes!"

They then asked, "What are your loves in your life?"

What an interesting question.

I responded, "I've got 5 loves in my life. I love God, I love my family, I love this great country, I love the NBA (specifically the Atlanta Hawks) and I love my career—in that order."

That individual looked a bit confused and asked, "Why?"

I said, "Well, it's easy. I am grateful for them, they contribute to my life, and I love them all. The first 3 obviously take care of themselves.

The NBA one is just my little vice, but really, when you want to know 'who' I am, it's about the people around me and those we serve."

I am fortunate enough to work for a company that wants desperately to give people permission to be who they really are and unlock a key to success that will help them change the world. Yes, we are in the sales business. Yes, we manufacture products. But as far as I am concerned, we are *really* here to serve, and in the service business, we are who we are . . . we are *servants!*

I do have those 5 loves in my life, and I am passionate about telling people about them and The Perfect Plan, but most important of all, I am Grateful and Thankful towards the people I serve.

It was there in the beginning. It was there all along, and now we understand why.

The original hypothesis was too radical to get the attention it deserved, but was actually proven true through a study that was never intended to be.

In the end, it was true.

It was a Perfect Plan.

Chapter 10

Closing Remarks

Who We Are and What We Believe

For the last 25 years, I have been in the sales business. I have never hidden the fact that my career is based on sales, largely on institutional financial sales and almost always large retirement plans. Sounds sexy, huh? Well, the retirement industry might not make the list of the world's most desirable careers for college graduates, but when they stumble into it, it's unreal.

I actually found my way into the world of institutional finance shortly after that night, 25 years ago, in New Orleans with my old boss. He encouraged me into sales because he had always admired the fact that marketing folks could control their own schedules. That sounded good enough for me, so I took his advice and dove into the deep end as fast as I could.

Since then, I have been serving people by selling employee benefit plans. It all started in 1987 while selling health insurance plans to small companies. Today, many of the world's largest and most desirable companies are, and have been my clients. Today, I am fortunate to have had many years where we have averaged $1 billion in annual sales.

I have changed firms a few times during my career, each move based on personal growth and where I felt my skills were taking me. I never left a firm for any reason other than growth. I am grateful to have worked for some of the top firms on Wall Street and in the financial industry. I still have friends at all of them. I even provide complimentary Perfect Plan training for them since, in their own way, they each contributed to the revelation that began all those years ago.

In 2001, I was employed by what I considered to be one of the world's finest organizations, MetLife. It was, and still is, a dynamic little fortune 100 company that is known for its insurance and financial products as well as their association with Charles Schultz's famous Peanuts characters. During my time there, I became their top institutional sales representative, and my office grew to the point where we made up 27% of their national US production for their RS Division. I also had the pleasure of working with one of the world's finest CEO's, C. Robert Henrikson. He taught me more than I can give him credit for, and we spent a lot of evenings driving around Alabama 'practicing' for what would become at the time, the country's largest IPO. I also had the good fortune of working with some of the best sales management teams and professionals available, especially with MetLife's Vice President of International Sales, Tim Mitchell. Without knowing it, Tim set the Perfect Plan on its foundation.

Tim can see and understand cultures and personalities better than anyone I have ever known. He is a friend to anyone in the room, and his strategic mind has the ability to understand human behavior at a level that transcends anything or anyone I have ever met. In the fall of 2001 when the US economy was in turmoil and the world was gripped with fear and rage, Tim came to me with an idea that would connect deeply with the work I had begun for the Perfect Plan a few months prior. His idea would conveniently couple with the Perfect Plan and will one day lead to what I feel will ultimately change the way we communicate, offer our services, and even set the policies that regulates world trade.

I was in my office that day when Tim approached me with a proposition that was hidden inside a question. "Do you think there might be a common thread between the world's elite sales people . . . regardless of what they sell?"

Wow, I thought, *what an interesting idea and eerily similar to the "radical" hypothesis I had developed at the beach on July 4th.*

I have always believed that there are no coincidences in life, and his timing was perfect. One of my favorite Mark Twain quotes puts it in perspective:

"Coincidences are God's way of remaining anonymous".

Tim had both the coolest and most challenging job in the world. He managed a sales force that touched almost every continent, and he was responsible for shaping all of them into the MetLife way of doing business. He had to do it by not disrupting the local culture, a task that frequently looked impossible. I was first introduced to Tim at a meeting in Mexico, and we quickly became friends. I had no idea how lucky I was at the time, because Tim is the kind of person everyone needs to know. He has a beautiful family, 4 lovely kids, and 3+ grandchildren, and he also has a lot of class—something you just can't buy or even learn. Tim just has it.

One of the things that made Tim so unique is his special way of seeing things in 3D, a skill that allowed him to understand what really drives behavior. That fall, his simple question evolved into a lot more than a mere lunchtime chat.

Tim had started to recognize that great sales people, all over the world, had similar tendencies, and he asked me if I wanted to take a closer look at them. In hind sight, and after a few lengthy late night discussions, I now know that the reason he came to me was because not only did he himself possess these qualities, but he recognized that my team did as well. We were quick to realize that the inertia already growing with the Perfect Plan study was the forum we needed to take the next steps.

With the help of two awesome interns, Mary Margret Surdo and Elizabeth Beck, we started what we thought was a simple summer MNE (Multi National Enterprise) paper. This became our first glimpse into a mystery we never knew existed and gave us the keys to solving it. *We found the evidence we needed to justify our reasoning, and prove the hypothesis.*

The girls spent the summer building databases on India's buying culture, while I spent the summer serving, writing papers, and selling institutional retirement plans. In my spare time, I was reading and interpreting the data. I also enjoyed a few international trips that allowed me to work alongside, some of the world's best and brightest sales people. It was exciting and full of the richest debates I have ever experienced. From market commentary in Europe to my concerns over a slower than expected middle class growth in China, we covered it all. Once the girls had finished their work and I injected my thoughts, we ultimately presented it to Tim and his team of advisors. From there, it was off to the races, and the search for the Perfect Plan hit light speed.

We first began testing the Perfect Plan in Monterey Mexico, and Mexico City where we were exposed to some of the finest marketing and sales people I had ever met. They didn't know it at the time, but they were to become our first test subjects. What we learned would ultimately help us discover the process that we would eventually test upon ourselves.

At the end of summer, we were already leading the nation and possibly the industry in domestic sales, and by the time we were done with our experiments, we had lapped the field. We hit our goals only 2 months into each annual cycle, and the company had to rethink their definition of the term 'capacity.'

We came to prove that 'capacity' was self-induced and sales goals were meaningless.

Using the Perfect Plan, we set and broke records faster than management could record them in their books and budgets.

The hypothesis was proven and we had successfully proven it ourselves. Best of all, we survived and were hungry for more challenges. This was something greater than the short term output that comes from a quick burst of focused and driven work. We thrived on it, we never lost energy, and never stopped to catch our breath—we did not need to.

The process and the Plan were so perfect that we actually created energy and desire from within.

We came to realize that most corporate middle managers drive toward the center of a bell curve that reflects a traditional sales training methodology. The challenge was that the "text book" method had not been challenged in over 100 years.

All innovative thinking and great ideas have detractors. For some it may be a natural resistance to change or fear of failure, while others see it as a challenge to their own limited success. In a few, it is a simple reflection of their own incompetence fueled by the desire to rise to fame while preventing anyone else from rising higher than themselves. Sadly, this isn't an economical rise they are trying to squash, but a childish need to suppress others from growing when they themselves have stalled. It is just the way life is, and these folks have been around for thousands of years. I suspect they will be here for thousands more.

These folks are a prime example of what Dr. Laurence J. Peter and Raymond Hull formulated in their 1969 book, *The Peter Principle.* In short, everyone, given enough upward mobility, will rise to the level of their incompetence—and there is plenty of *that* in the world. If you don't believe it, just look at Congress these days.

The Peter Principle happens in a lot of sales management decisions by those who don't want to unlock their team's full potential for fear that they will lose control over them.

You know this is happening, because the managers and senior executives who have risen far beyond their training and capabilities are forced to rethink the leadership of their own teams. This too is nothing new.

Before Peter and Hull's treatise on the subject, a similar experience was described as early as 1767 by Gotthold Ephraim Lessing in his comedy, *Minna von Barnhelm.* When translated from German to English, it tells of his own conclusions regarding his rise to leadership: "To become more than a sergeant? I don't consider it. I am a good sergeant; I might easily make a bad captain, and certainly a worse general. People have had this experience."

It is a principle that, like the Perfect Plan, spans the ages and is true and relevant in any era. In order to truly succeed and feel the powerful results unlocked within the Perfect Plan, there needs to be an environment committed to success and the success of everyone on the team. No egos or fear, just sincere desire to see others grow to their fullest potential, even if it might seem greater than one's own.

We knew about this concept, and we were aware of some outside resistance building to the Perfect Plan, but it really only became evident a few years later. After years of study, Billions of dollars in record breaking sales, and millions of miles traveled, I had decided to leave MetLife. It was then, and has been to this day the single most difficult professional decision of my career. To leave a firm that I admired so much, and one whose leadership was so committed to everyone's success, was questioned by everyone I knew both personally and professionally. I had a simple reason for leaving, and as I had mentioned before, I don't believe in coincidences. My decision to leave was not a reflection on MetLife's leadership at all. In fact, I miss working with them every day, and who wouldn't? From Tim Mitchell and Rob Henrikson to other legendary greats like Bill Topetta, Brian Fox, George Castineiras, John Morabitto, and the great Bob BenMoche, I have enjoyed working with and miss working with these dynamic and passionate individuals who only ever offered their best to everyone on their teams.

I was standing in the town square of old Prague in the Czech Republic when I felt that I was called to a new organization. One, who at the time, had similar leadership, values and desires to that of MetLife. It was a great organization who wanted growth but would soon find themselves adrift and caught in a classic Peter Principle rift. As a result of retirements and organizational changes, a new management team intruded in such a way as to lead them to forget their passions and allow egos to interfere. They were stalling, and it was into this meltdown that I felt compelled to jump. While there were times when I questioned the reasons I was drawn there, I soon realized that for a hypothesis and project as life altering as the Perfect Plan to grow, it must first be tested. I tested it there.

Win the Lobster

Even though the climate quickly grew stale and the changes occurring at the new firm were uncomfortable, I had the pleasure of briefly working alongside one of the greatest sales managers of all time, George Sutherland.

George was the type of guy that everyone in sales needs. He was a combination friend, therapist, and motivator while exuding Yoda-like wisdom and mentorship. He had been to a few 'rodeos' in his career and was 100% committed to putting others ahead of himself. He followed all of the Perfect Plan principles before he even knew they existed. He would become our greatest test subject, and he willingly gave his time and talent without any expectation of anything in return. George was the best, and he wanted everyone to outgrow him. He felt that the more mini-Yoda's he could reproduce, the better the world would become, and he was right!

Under George's leadership, I soon came to realize that once the Perfect Plan was in place, all we had to do was spread the word. I knew what it was capable of doing. We just had to implement it, and once we did, our teams once again became successful beyond anyone's wildest dreams. The impact was felt on so many levels. At first, we showed results faster than anyone in the US market thought possible as we drove sales to exceed the $1 billion dollar mark. That was just the beginning. Soon the real 'test' came and we pushed things to the brink as a team and as individuals.

The first real live test came at a sales training conference in Charlotte that would become famous and infamous at the same time. It was harmless and lots of fun, but looking back I came to realize the significance of the thought processes that were revealed by the other teams. It was a glimpse into the future.

We were sent to Charlotte to learn and train under an outside sales consultant who I quickly began to appreciate and admire. He was not the typical trainer who asked you to recite the ABC's of sales (Always Be Closing). Instead, he looked at the world though a different light. He was more concerned about how you looked to a buyer and the technical impact of your 'style' on the audience and decision makers than he was about what it was that you were selling. He put us through two days of interactive sessions and even filmed the way we stood, talked and moved in front of our buyers. It was obvious that the next few days would be enlightening and a bit exciting.

On the last day, he let us know that we would be divided into teams so as to role play our presentation skills in front of our management team who had flown into town to witness the results. He would supply the topic, and we had to present and hypothetically 'sell' to the management team who would play the part of a buying committee. To motivate us, he made it into a competition. Every team would make a presentation in front of the judges who would adjust their 'character' as they saw fit in order to push us to the brink of our skill sets. The judges would then decide upon a winner and that's where the fun began. However, it soon became brutally honest that the winning team would be held in great admiration and all others would be referred to simply as 'losers.'

The winning team would be judged on their skills and what they had learned from the previous day's efforts. The winning team would also be awarded a special prize. The "best of the best" would receive a pair of live Maine lobsters sent to their home. They would also get all the matching compliments of a fine lobster dinner including clam chowder, fresh corn and even a Boston cream pie.

Oh yes, this would be fun.

The problem was that the management team they sent was partially made up of the same executives that were responsible for turning the company's culture upside down in ego driven self-destruction. Each had technically risen in the ranks to the level of their incompetence and they wanted to judge us . . . the creative guys.

I quickly came to realize that this was not going to be fun.

At the time, the task seemed simple enough for me and my team. Win the lobsters! Little did we know that the judges brought in from our Home Office had another plan in mind. They wanted to see if our team could survive once we were separated, so they forced a new group of team members on me who were as far from the Perfect Plan as anyone could get. They were without question really nice people, but their skill sets were based on classical techniques and even worse, trained by a management team who must have been Larry Peter's original test group. They maximized the Peter Principle in every possible way—even to the point of wanting to compromise everyone else's successes in order to feed their own egos. It was beginning to look like a long day.

As we broke up into our new teams, we were given our assignment which included the topic and the order in which we would be presenting. Our assignment was silly in its predictability because we drew a very difficult institutional type of sale. The only hint at any good news was that we drew the longest stick and were awarded the very last slot to present.

The corporate newbie's assigned to my team thought our drawn lot was great, but I knew we had been set up. The judges wanted us to present last so as to be in front of the *entire* class along, plus a host of other dignitaries they had brought to the meeting. It was, in essence, equivalent to a public hanging spectacle, but they underestimated us. They had given me enough time to whip them into shape, so to speak—15 minutes to be exact.

As I sat down with the team to guide and direct them to success, it became apparent how tough they wanted to make it. Like a fountain, they spouted out countless regiments of text book sales steps that would have been revolutionary only in the Dark Ages. They wanted to 'probe' the client—a concept I find terrifying—and then create a 'disturbance' with the client's current situation so the said client could be 'motivated' to buy . . . ouch. It was quickly clear that I needed to take control and put things into perspective. In the end, the only thing their methodology would create is a new name tag that read 'loser' on it.

I quickly took over by asking them about our goals, and I was shocked at their answers. Each wanted to actually present a 'sale' to these "hypothetical" Board of Directors and to follow predefined steps in closing the deal. They were eager and excited, but unfortunately, they were also being led by their own bosses to the slaughter.

I listened to them the best I could and even took notes in order to appear engaged, but it came to the point where I had to step in and stop the nonsense. I asked them a few simple questions and was satisfied that they were willing to take direction. I asked them to describe how they as a team were motivated to 'nudge' the client to select us as the product of choice. They were speechless. My question didn't follow their preprogrammed set of steps. To get them 'on track' with the Perfect Plan, I needed to get them 'off track' first. In other words, I needed to reprogram them.

So I asked another simple question, "What do you personally want to achieve in this exercise?" No one seemed to know, so I gave them the answer, "I want to win the lobsters!" Yes, win the lobsters. In fact, not only should they be motivated to win the lobsters, but they should want to win it by the largest margin in the competition's history. They should be prepared to celebrate like there is no tomorrow when they get home and find the lobsters on their doorsteps. Success in this case was not about following a technical path—we certainly could not 'sell' anything to a hypothetical board or improperly motivated set of buyers—but we could win the lobsters. That was what this was really all about. They quickly became motivated.

They then spent the next 7 minutes (the rest of our prep time) receiving the world's fasted crash course on the Perfect Plan. I convinced them that if they followed the simple steps I had outlined for them, our odds of winning were better than they could imagine. Each sat on the edge of their seats, took notes and opened their minds like the professionals they would soon grow to become. This handpicked, midlevel team of Peter Principle poster children had begun a process that would not only plant the seeds of change in their own lives, but the seeds of their future and the incredibly successful careers they would come to enjoy.

For the first time, I began to see what would happen when the Perfect Plan was tested in adversity. I knew that I had been set up to fail by a group of middle managers who would judge by perception and would rather see others fail than grow themselves, but I jumped for joy when I saw what was beginning to happen. My little team of underdogs began to actually reverse their own paths, opening up to a new idea they found to be revolutionary. In less than 10 minutes, they were exposed to the Perfect Plan and clearly focused on the goal of winning the lobsters. They trusted me, and we walked into the room ready for victory.

I was thrilled to see their actions that afternoon. They were flawless in delivering their presentation and they followed the Perfect Plan . . . well, perfectly. We were so good that not only did we miss our own hanging, but those same judges who had set us up to fail gave us a perfect score. The proctor told us later that it was the first perfect score he had ever seen in his 20+ year career! The team was exceptional.

The Perfect Plan had worked when tested, true, but it had done so much more than that. It had elevated some folks to a level and in a way that I hoped would continue indefinitely.

The Perfect Plan won, and it had won big.

It was not just the lobsters that defined us, it was the test against adversity that caused the victory note to sound so clear. I know that the win that day was nothing compared to similar victories the Plan had achieved in the past, but the triumph was huge and the proof undeniable.

The Perfect Plan would be tested several times again, and before long another change was in store for me. This time, it was a change of celebration, and it seemed like everything was heading to where it was always meant to be. It was going home, and even it was never part of the goal, the original "radical" hypothesis was proven true.

So there it was . . . a story that began with a simple idea.

It was proven by a test, ridiculed by a trial, and survived on its truth.

It not only survived, it grew beyond all expectations. The proof was clear with billions of dollars in sales, growth more than anyone had ever dreamed possible.

In the end, it is a message that would help others in ways we never could envision.

It was *perfect*.

A Few Who Make Up the Top 1%

Every year, we recognize the companies and individuals who are not only in the 1% club, but represent all 6 principles of the Perfect Plan. This is not for those who have endorsed the Perfect Plan, but a chance for us to endorse them! They are the best of the best and live to *serve*. Some were in the original test groups and others are discovered through random acts and long term relations. Either way, they are the best and we want to recognize them for their work—not just today, but every day and for every life they touch.

The 2012 Standouts

- ❖ **Ritz Carlton**
- ❖ **Chick-fil-A**
- ❖ **Mathew Tollison—Ridgeworth Investments**
- ❖ **Henssler Financial**
- ❖ **The MG Group of Merrill Lynch**
- ❖ **James Laschinger**
- ❖ **Alex Grigorian—InterContinental Hotel Group**
- ❖ **David Griffin**
- ❖ **North Point Ministries**
- ❖ **The Scheduling Institute**
- ❖ **Triumph Motorcycles**
- ❖ **Brian Fox—MetLife**
- ❖ **US Army Rangers**

- ❖ JonPaul's
- ❖ Clark Howard
- ❖ American Century Investments
- ❖ OneAmerica Financial Partners
- ❖ CCCi

Exemplifying the Principle of Gratification

Ritz Carlton—"It's my pleasure."

Not many in today's world can openly express their heartfelt desire to serve better than the folks at Ritz Carlton. Their 5 star hotels represent a hundred years of exemplary service which is focused solely on their guests. Their motto says it all: "We are Ladies and Gentlemen serving Ladies and Gentlemen." One of the most outward acts of gratification occurs when a Ritz Carlton employees receives a simple, "Thank you," from a guest. When they reply, it is never with the customary, "You're welcome," but with their signature statement, "It's my pleasure."

At the Ritz Carlton, they realize that it is a pleasure to serve others and they are not afraid to say it, or believe it. Their simple act of gratification sets them apart with sincerity like no others. When people ask what it takes to be in the Top 1%, it's easy to direct them to the Ritz Carlton way of doing business and its foundational belief that serving others is not and act or deed, but a pleasure.

Chick-fil-A—Every Life Has a Story

In 1946 when Truett Cathy opened his first restaurant, he had one thing in mind. Oddly enough, it was not about fast food, but about "quick service." He also set the tone by deciding not to be open on Sundays. It was, in their words, as much of a practical decision as it was spiritual. Truett always wanted to thank his employees by giving them a day to rest. This allows them to spend time with family and friends as well as worship where they pleased. By showing his gratitude for over 60 years, Chick-fil-A has become one of the world's leading restaurants, and their corporate giving is in a field all to itself.

While great business management and good decisions continues to lead the company to become a great powerhouse in their market, it is really about their service to others and the way they see the world. A few years ago, one of the greatest training videos of all-time hit the social media world and allowed the outside to glimpse into the wonderful and grateful world of a Chick-fil-A employee. If you want to see what real gratification is in today's world, search for the video, and you will be amazed and humbled: *Every Life Has a Story*. It will change the way you see the world, and allow you into why they understand "gratification" and service.

Mathew Tollison—Ridgeworth Investments

When we were going deep into the minds of the world's best, it always amazed us when the "brand" of an organization became part of a personality or that of a single human being. Matthew Tollison was an early test subject of our Perfect Plan because not only did he represent the Top 1%, but his corporate gratitude toward his employer made it an exponential factor. When a person of Matthew's skill and commitment to serve is combined with a firm who has equal focus and drive, it becomes magical.

Matthew is what others want to be, a servant who is grateful and creates the 'Attitude of Gratitude' wherever he is in the world. He is often the leader of business sessions and conferences, but unlike others who try to keep everything to themselves, Matthew generates activity and appreciation for everyone in the room, even with his competitors. Matthew was once heard saying, "I discovered a long time ago that the pie of opportunity is greater than anyone can ever get to, so why not share it with everyone and cheer for their success as well . . . I am just grateful for the opportunity to serve." Wow!

Exemplifying the Principle of Education

Henssler Financial—From College Students to Wall Street

Dr. Gene Henssler earned his PhD in Finance from the University of Michigan and taught at Georgia State University, University of Toledo and Grand Valley State University in Michigan. In 1986 he became a Professor of Finance at Kennesaw State University, taking an early retirement in 1996. Today, Dr. Henssler holds the title of Professor Emeritus of Finance at Kennesaw State University, but that's just the beginning.

Gene was one of the original variables that helped lead us to the 1% by teaching us that school should never stand in the way of anyone's education. His ability to take the most complex subjects and help someone understand the situation with confidence and new found pride, separates him from the pack. Once he realized that he could teach outside the traditional walls of a classroom, he became a pioneer in radio financial talk shows by talking to people and radio audiences like they were his best friend. His ability to transform others and lead them into a better path has made him a regular on some of the nation's most respected TV News and radio shows. He has founded the Henssler Financial Center at Kennesaw State University and funded it with "real dollars" so students can experience the markets and learn in true to life form. In the end, Dr. Henssler sets the stage and delivers with his famous motto: "Live Ready" No one does that better than Dr. Gene Henssler.

The MG Group of Merrill Lynch—Where the World Comes Together

The MG is made up of a fascinating slice of culture, academic power, and most impressively, friends. Alvaro Galvis, Fred Mannheimer, Sean Foote, Stephen Welch, and Kelly Meneses were born worlds apart, but came together to help make Merrill Lynch one of the most successful firms on the planet. Their team is clearly the perfect representation of how the Top 1% run their lives, by serving and educating others.

"We are acutely aware that most people retain very little of what you say to them in a presentation," Alvaro explained, "so it is our job to be educated in a way that they can outsource their success to us." As international finance experts and a leading marketing firm of US based retirement plans, they know that their clients really don't want to know everything they do. That is why they hire the MG Group. "We know, accept, and welcome their trust," Fred said. "They need to be running their business, not worrying about their retirement plan." Their creed is simple: "Let us do that for you."

Sean and Stephen both represent a special piece of their team's success. "Through our education, we can serve them best, and help them get to a better place" Sean said.

Stephen likes to point out that "Sometimes, education is not about 'learning,' but about 'knowing' that the ones serving you have it covered. It is what we pride ourselves on." The MG Group performs at the highest level, knowing that it is never about them, but for those they serve. Through real education, they deliver something above the other 99%—trust.

James Laschinger—Where a Dashboard First Found a Boardroom

What happens when a tennis prodigy and NCAA Champion meets Wall Street? He builds a Dashboard of course. James Laschinger, or 'J' as he is known, was built for athletic success, but few saw the future as well as he did—and still does today. "I knew that my ability to play tennis at the University of Georgia would afford me the education I would need to serve others." It was just a matter of time before the NCAA Arthur Ashe Award winner would make his mark off the court and stamp it on Wall Street.

J has always known that people are auditory, and in many cases, they understand what is being told to them better than what they can read for themselves. This is what led J to create one of the first financial dashboards. "I wanted to help my clients make educated decisions about very complex issues without requiring them to become the expert, because that's why they hire me." J is always the first to give credit to his clients, but also delivers educational excellence at a level that impresses even others in the Top 1%. As one of the original test subjects, J opened his practice to us and brought us into a world where sports and Wall Street met in a way that allowed everyone to participate. "I work hard to create reports that are so simple to read. Everyone walks away having made a good decision and the ability to justify their vote."

J's clients are some of the most recognized brands in the world and all appreciate his ability to educate them in a way where they can maintain their focus without being caught in the massive amounts of detail. "I want them to run their business and not have to worry about the daily in and out movements of the stock markets. I also want them to understand and be informed. That is why I created the Dashboard . . . now everyone can make good decisions."

J took his championship ability to the world, but not focused on winning it for himself, but helping others be champions as well. By serving others with education, J teaches everyone that you hold a trophy the highest when it is held for others.

Exemplifying the Principle of Ease of Business

InterContinental Hotels—Alex Grigorian "Live Deliberately"

While Dr. Henssler was building a platform of 'living ready,' Alex Grigorian was "living deliberately" in a place few could imaging today. Growing up in Soviet controlled Armenia meant that you became subject to authority and forced to live as they dictated your life. "It was a tough time," Alex admitted. It is hard for most people to imagine living in a world where it was illegal to listen to western music—even the Beatles! "We would hide in a closet late at night with a flash light and a faded picture of Paul McCartney, listening to tapes that were bootlegged into the country." It seems like a distant memory, but it was just 20 years ago when Alex and his wife slipped out of Armenia with a dream of freedom and the passion to live a better life.

"I am so blessed, it goes beyond words," said Alex, who is now the Senior Vice President of IT for one of the world's largest hotel chains, IHG. "My job is unbelievable and I love it more every day!" he said. "My goal is to make sure your life is simple and easy by insuring the systems (reservations, rewards, all technology really) works, so you, our guests, and our customers don't have to worry or think about anything." This is why Alex represents the Top 1%, not because of his passion to live himself, but his passion to allow you to "outsource your successful trip" to him. Alex knows, like Steve Jobs before him, that "genius is making things simpler," not by adding things on to your already busy life. The unique thing about Alex is that in living deliberately, he allows others to understand and know that, wherever they are anywhere around the world, his systems have them covered.

Alex has always been a 1%'er, even in those darker days of Soviet oppression. "I know that every day is a wonderful day, no matter what your circumstances are, so if I can help and make it better, that's what I will do."

Alex is committed to living deliberately and helping tens of thousands of people "know" that their lives will be easier today, "deliberately"

David Griffin—CS001

David Griffin holds a special place in Perfect Plan history by being tagged CS001, or Case Study #1. We were first magnetized to David when he was a recent college graduate, making his way into the corporate world. We met with David by accident, but we instantly knew he was different. His genuine charm and desire to serve others was coupled with a personality that resembled the fictional persona in the wonderful Dos Equis ad campaign: "the Most Interesting Man in the World." Only he had achieved it years before the famous commercial had aired.

David has a simple philosophy that separated him at an early age from the others. He believes in service that makes people's lives easier by freeing them with the truth. "I learned at an early age, that people don't need more work or crisis in their lives, they are actually seeking an easier place to live and work . . . that's why they hire me." David goes on to explain that the best way to make anyone's life better is by helping them find the truth in whatever their situation might be. To ease someone's burden, you have to discover the reason for their distraction before you can set them on a course to freedom. That process involves creating an environment that is inviting to everyone and their cause. He welcomes them with open arms and solves their problems in a way that puts everyone at ease. "I never want to expose an issue with negative or painful emotions, people have enough of that in their lives without bringing it to their work" he said. "I focus on making their lives easier by helping them understand that we can work together to make complex issues simple, and therefore their lives will be at peace."

It's easy for the original case study and always has been. Now that's "interesting!"

North Point Ministries—If It Looks Easy, It's Not

What is Andy Stanley and North Point Ministries secret to serving over 30,000 people every Sunday? Simple, make it look easier than it really is, and to them, that's why they exist.

In 1995, a vision was set forth that changed the way Churches look, feel, and most importantly, "serve." It revolved around an idea that focused on creating an environment where everyone, even those who never attended a Church before, would love to go and spend time. That ultimately became the foundation upon which tens of thousands came to attend a weekly event. It has the same feel as attending a play or a movie. You never have to worry about being judged or having to act or live a certain way. That's when the magic happens! As the program begins, everyone feels compelled to participate in a way that works best for them. The audience environment is similar to doing a wave at a football game—it is fun, exciting, and everyone can do it. Before long, you find yourself enjoying some of the world's elite musicians, singing everything from Michael Jackson songs to

ESPN's Sports Center theme. Nothing is out of reach when it comes to creating the world's most magnetizing environment for everyone to enjoy. Though it may look easy, it is not.

Every week, hundreds of employees and volunteers come together to make your experience so easy that you never notice the sheer volume of people, cars, and logistics necessary to move 30,000 in and out of a location with a one hour turn around. The focus and energy that goes into making every person's experience "easy", is nothing short of miraculous. From the parking lot attendants and greeters to their state of the art IT and video, the attendees are totally relaxed as they experience one of the greatest speakers in history, Andy Stanley, deliver a message of hope and love to people here, there, and everywhere. Best of all, it is easy . . . for you that is.

Exemplifying the Principle of Create—
Don't Compete

Jay Geier's The Scheduling Institute—The Best of the Best

Growth at 5x? 10x? Where do you want to be?

That's the question Jay Geier asks all of his clients. "Where do you want to be? I will help you get there."

The energy is off the chart and Jay creates a sensation that, in his words, "transforms teams." Jay recognized years ago that we are all here to create and serve, so why not help others by bringing them together to grow at exponential rates by getting back to the basics. The Scheduling Institute is designed to help small and medium size medical and dental practices grow to their fullest potential. Their revolutionary technology and methodology takes a seemingly static environment and magnetizes them by giving them "permission" to grow and change.

What makes Jay and his team of 75+ employees special is their understanding of human behavior and their acceptance that everyone is different. "If you can discover how someone is wired, it opens the door for you to communicate and train them in a way that will allow them to reach their ultimate achievement," said Jay. "We are all different, so treating everyone the same obviously does not work." That's where the brilliance of the Scheduling Institute kicks in. They serve over 4,000 practices nationwide by creating environments where the team discovers an unquenchable desire to thrive and grow together. "We want to make sure we are creating an environment for everyone to maximize their team and grow at a rate of 5x or 10x, wherever they are comfortable, but it all starts with a single step."

Special note: The Scheduling Institute ranked number 1 in the Perfect Plan study for the principle of Create—Don't Compete, but it also scored top 5 in every other category. In fact, within the world's Top 1%, many on staff believe that Jay Geier and his organization has gone where no one else has ever been, and possibly ranked in the top 1% of the world's 1%—truly phenomenal.

Triumph Motorcycles—Where "Cool" Meets the Top 1%

As the Perfect Plan study took our teams around the world to meet the best of the best, it quickly became apparent that the Top 1% rarely found fame outside their nucleus of work. In fact, most of the case subjects were rarely known outside of their immediate environment or those whom they served, but that was not true for this company. As we came to know Triumph and their work, it quickly became apparent that they were not only building some of the world's best motorcycles, they were also building a culture.

For over 100 years, the brand Triumph has been associated with a culture and lifestyle that surpasses their product and that of the competition. When we began to dissect and study their phenomenon, we realized that they were much more than a product, because their creativity was impacting a culture. While there are certainly other great brands in the motorcycle world, we discovered that something special happened when anyone would mention Triumph, and the verbal response was always the same: "Cool." When we tested this unusual response, we quickly discovered why this incredible magnetism worked.

Steve McQueen, Fonzie, Marlon Brando in *The Wild Ones*, Ann Margaret, Angelina Jolie, Harrison Ford, the Matrix movie characters, Clint Eastwood, and even Elvis—all iconic figures in culture have one thing in common. They rode Triumph motorcycles.

In the process of creating and building one of the world's finest products, Triumph decided not to compete with other manufacturers, but to create an icon for the ages. In doing so, they secured themselves in the Top 1% club by focusing on a magnetism that transformed multiple generations while remaining timeless in their spirit. We learned that here is a lot more to Triumph than motorcycles, and we are excited to see what they will do over the next 100 years or so.

That's cool.

MetLife and Brian Fox—Life at its Best

MetLife is without question one of the largest firms represented on the Perfect Plans list of the Top 1%, and that makes it all the more special. One thing we discovered that prevented several companies from moving into the top 1% was their size. In many cases, a company's size had become so cumbersome, that it's like trying to control a teenage dinosaur—the desire is there, but asking something of such proportion to change directions and focus is an entirely different thing. Thankfully for MetLife and their Chief Marketing Officer, Brian Fox, that is not the case for one of America's most distinguished and historical firms.

In 1908, MetLife built the tallest building in the world, as some reporters wrote, literally "scraping the sky". When it was completed, MetLife placed a light on its top for the entire world to see, but little did they realize how impactful that light would become as it served history in more ways than they could have ever imagined. From housing the survivors of the Titanic, to becoming the nation's largest buyer of bonds during WWII, MetLife began creating opportunities for America that spanned beyond typical insurance and became a synergy for creativity that would change the world. As the largest backer of American farm mortgages during the Great Depression to the first to use computers in the 1950's, MetLife consistently found ways to create opportunities instead of focusing on their competitors.

"We have always sought to do the right thing and create solutions beyond our product offerings" says Brian Fox, CMO and member of the Top 1% club himself. "While we absolutely *love* our relationship with the famous Peanuts characters, we also enjoy impacting people's lives around the globe in ways few ever know." One such moment happened on a beautiful, crisp, blue sky morning in September of 2001.

"September 11th was a dark day for us at MetLife," said Fox. "We lost a lot of great people that morning, and their legacy will be with us forever." As anyone who has ever seen a picture of New York City knows, MetLife is a fixture in the city's skyline, towering above Grand Central Station with a marquee for everyone to see. As open as they are about their presence in NYC, few people get to go inside the hearts and minds of the senior management teams at MetLife. If you could have, you might have understood their desire to create a new beginning that day in 2001 for the city and ultimately America. "It was never a hard decision for us to do the right thing," explained Brian. "Our CEO at the time never hesitated as we immediately began pumping money back into the US economy by flushing $1 billion cash into the stock markets to help shore up the economy, which was crippled by the attacks."

MetLife also did something no one would have ever guessed, as Brian tells with a warm and enduring smile, "We immediately began paying life insurance claims for the victims of the attacks, and we never hesitated." The wonderful thing about this act is that they never required death certificates or any real proof that the victims were lost, they simply paid the claims.

"MetLife has always done the right thing and we always will. It is built into the heritage and the core of our people to serve others and create opportunities from our vast resources to go beyond products, investments, and properties."

Some of MetLife's success is rooted in their focus to be the best by never having "hobbies." As Brian and others likes to say, "If we can't be #1 or #2 in a particular market space, there is no need to try, because we are not in the 'hobby' business, but in the service business."

Brian said, "We serve, by being the best we can be, and that allows us to unleash our creativity and in turn provide resources, capital, and even aid when people need it most."

Brian is a third generation MetLife employee and loves every second of it. "I wake up every day and run to my office," he said with unbridled enthusiasm. "Where else can I live in such a creative environment serving others, while surrounded with the world's best and brightest minds all focused on being the best you can be? What a blessing!"

Brian has been one of the Top 1% for a long time, and his work within MetLife guarantees MetLife's status in the same category for years to come.

Exemplifying the Principle of the Value is Greater than the Cost

US Army Rangers—Rangers Lead the Way

We have to admit that when the study began, seeking to discover the secrets to the world's best in sales and marketing, we never thought it would lead us where it did, but the US Army Rangers 75th Ranger Regiment stationed in Ft. Benning and Hunter Air Field quickly became the story behind the real meaning of the Perfect Plan.

The US Army Rangers date back as early as the 17th century, but were first organized in the American Revolutionary War. They have fought to defend the world's freedom for over 200 years and continue representing the bravest among us today. While we never thought to study them in the beginning, they won the unanimous vote as the Top 1% in this particular principle without anyone having to question or ask why.

While spending time with them among their ranks and leadership, we found that they epitomize the concept of a value being greater than the price. In their situation, the "price" is more than what most people are willing to pay. "Every day, there is a Ranger sleeping in the mud, putting his life on the line somewhere thousands of miles from home, so you can live in peace," said Richard Schooley, one of the founders of Sua Sponte—the Rangers support charity based in Savannah Georgia. "We live to serve them, knowing they are volunteering to serve us making the ultimate sacrifice every day," said their biggest supporter, David Ermer.

The US Army Rangers are an elite group of soldiers who offer an unprecedented value with their service that for us, should outweigh the cost, but as others have also done in history, they offer to pay the price for you. RLTW

JonPaul's—European Tradition Comes to America

A few years ago, a famous American credit card company ran an ad campaign entitled "priceless." It focused on the times in your life where you look back and realize the moment had a value that exceeded every expectation, hence it is "priceless." The commercials implied that these moments were few and far between, so you had better be ready, and their company was there to help you prepare. Fortunately for the rest of the world, someone had a different take of the idea.

Dr. JonPaul Leskie received his PhD in Computer Science from the University of California before he spent a few years at MIT working on some really cool stuff. He touched everything from the world's leading telecommunication companies to Home Land Security—no doubt possessing a few secrets in his head. Thankfully for the world, JonPaul is a good guy, and better yet, as one of the world's Top 1%, he thinks a little out of the box. "Why should you have to wait for those priceless moments in life?" he said. "Why not make it happen whenever you want it to"

The idea came to him one day in Europe as he went to get a haircut and experienced something magical. His experience prompted him to ask, "What would a man pay if he could schedule time away from the world [to be] in utter peace for an hour every other week or so to recharge, relax, and be served by some of the world's best professionals?"

He knew the buyers pyramid and recognized that time and the return on times investment was the driving decision among the "C Suite," so he created the ultimate experience with a value greater than the price.

Everyone gets a haircut these days, and conveniently enough, his wife Cathy is not only a master barber, but one of the world's most unique personalities! "It really is the 'Cathy Show' here at JonPaul's," he said. It is where a gentleman can come in for an hour and a half to experience true relaxation with a traditional haircut, shave, facial, shoulder massage, shoe shine, and even a cocktail. All while they can relax or experience a little of Cathy's worldly therapy. "I always treat the guys right here, and I am so appreciative when they ask for my advice on things they can't ask their peers or co-workers about their business. CEO's and business owners are a lonely group, and if I can be here to help and lend a bit of advice, I am all for it." She says, "Running this business is not different from any others, so I can offer them a moment of relaxing service while they bounce ideas around while feeling great about their appearance when they leave."

Cathy has staffed the firm with ultimate professionals in men's grooming. From Theresa's deep tissue sports message to April's manicures, everything is offered from cigars to custom suites, accessories to styling products. It's a one stop shop for the guy who wants to step away for a moment and be served in a way that they deserve before they walk back into the world and face tomorrow's challenges. "The best part of JonPaul's," said frequent customer Dr. Burke Robinson, "is the value to price ratio." "I am always amazed that I can slip into such a wonderful place for around $50.00 and feel like I have been treated like a million dollars!" said retired CEO and Harvard Business School graduate Fred Erler.

Even better, JonPaul's is for everyone, especially if you are in the Atlanta area. You don't have to be a CEO, PhD, MD or business owner to appreciate the ultimate value and experience. JonPaul's is designed to serve everyone and has succeeded in creating a priceless moment that for once, can be scheduled.

Clark Howard—The Clark Howard Show

Clark is one of the top radio and TV personalities in the world today, and that's pretty special for such a regular guy. One of the reasons Clark was chosen as a stand out among the Top 1% was his connection with people and his acceptance of a unique responsibility. Clark understands that 85% of a decision is based on emotion and then justified with 15% of the facts, so Clark set out to help people with the "justification" portion of the formula.

"I want to help people save money," says Clark everyday on his nationally syndicated radio show. "We are here to serve and help people find the best deals as well as avoid getting ripped off." Best of all, Clark's services are free to everyone.

Whether you watch him on CNN's Headline News, visit his web site, or listen to him on any of 200 plus radio stations that broadcast his show every day, you quickly discover that Clark is the real thing.

Clark seems to be on TV 24 hours a day giving advice to anyone who wants to understand value. His show *Evening Express* airs live every weekday from 5-7 pm ET from HLN's world headquarters in Atlanta. He is also a TV reporter on Atlanta's ABC affiliate WSB-TV. As if that is not enough, Clark's weekly newspaper column in *The*

Atlanta Journal-Constituion is syndicated to multiple papers throughout the country.

It doesn't stop there, not only has he published 9 books on his favorite subject, he offers free advice 45 hours a week off the air through 145 volunteers all dedicated to serving others.

We first met Clark officially a few years ago when he accepted a last minute invitation to speak at a local Atlanta High Schools graduation. The original speaker cancelled at the last moment leaving the school with little hope to fill the slot. After a few calls and a local family connection, Clark jumped at the chance to fill in . . . but there was a little snag.

Clark's "fee" for public speaking at the time for private events was $15,000.00 an hour. While many find that expensive, those who know Clark and his message realize that that is a check well worth writing. In perfect "servants" fashion, it is always a pleasant surprise when people discover to whom you write the check if you want to hear Clark speak at your event—Habitat for Humanity. Wow! A guy who can command $15,000.00 an hour does not accept the checks, but ask that you write it directly to one of his favorite charities so you can help others have a home . . . Wow again!

When the High School Clark was scheduled to give their graduation speech heard about the fee, they were a worried at first, but made it work. They did it not by writing a check they could not afford *(by the way, Clark had told them not to worry about the $15k, but to do what they could)*, but they were so motivated by Clark that they volunteered to work all summer raising enough money to build a Habitat for Humanity home themselves, so they could serve others as well. Wow again and again, but there is more . . .

Clark was so moved by what these kids had agreed to do, that he took one more step toward serving others, in a way no one expected. While on stage and graciously hearing what the kids had announced they would accomplish for others, Clark raised the bar as only he could. Visibly moved by the kids kind act, Clark announced that he would match their generosity dollar-for-dollar and build a second Habitat for Humanity house along side of theirs (with his own money) in order to make the gift twice as impactful to a family in need.

Wow, Wow, Wow indeed.

By helping other justify value and save money, Clark teaches us how to serve. "The money you save is worthless unless you help others and make the world a better place" one of the kids was heard saying that summer. They are right, as Clark's education continues to impact others well beyond the piggy bank.

Exemplifying the Principle of Giving Forward

American Century Investments—Profits with a Purpose

Based in Kansas City, this may help explain why one of Wall Street's best known brands is actually one of the country's most forward giving and benevolent organization in the country. With a relatively simple understanding that they are from Main Street, not Wall Street, they can focus on their customer while helping them get to a better place.

Since 1958, American Century has been privately held and manages billions of dollars for their customers with a promise to always do it right, but it goes much deeper than that.

"American Century Investments is guided by core values that shape the way we conduct our business. These have been in place since 1958, when James E. Stowers Jr. founded the company and they have not changed" Says long time employee Bruce Caldwell

"These values include a strong commitment to helping others and building a strong community.

In 1994, Jim and Virginia Stowers, the company's founders, decided they wanted to give back something "more valuable than money" to the millions of people who helped make their success possible.

As cancer survivors themselves, Jim and Virginia, decided to focus on a way to improve the quality of others' lives so they, too, could survive. That is when they decided to create the Stowers Institute for

Medical Research—one of the most innovative biomedical research organizations in the world.

American Century to this day lives out the Stowers' model of giving something "more valuable than money" by strategically focusing its giving forward more than 40% of their profits to support research to help cure genetically-based diseases including cancer, diabetes, and dementia.

As with a select few, American Century grew with the luxury of having members of the Top 1% as owners, the Stowers family, within their ranks. Today, their leadership is keenly focused on giving forward and understanding that their existence helps folks beyond their product lines. CEO Jonathan Thomas is a passionate supporter of their mission: Profits with a Purpose. He works tirelessly to promote their work in order to help others find the hope of one day living cancer free. Their relationship with The LIVESTRONG Foundation is monumental and they forge ahead every day with a mission to help others survive. Surrounded with an elite executive team and a clear mission, they hope to exceed their client's expectations, but also change the world.

OneAmerica Financial Partners—Bigger Is Not Better; Better Is Better

When OneAmerica's CEO Dayton Molendorp first uttered the words, "Bigger is not better; better is better," it stuck.

With a commitment to be there when their clients need them most, the OneAmerica family of firms has built their 150+ year history on a culture of service, fueled by a "servant's heart." "We are big enough to matter, but small enough to care," said Bill Yoerger, the company's President and Divisional head. "We grow through hard work and commitment, but we never forget why," said senior executive Mark Glavin. "We are here to serve."

There seem to be countless examples of the company's commitment to give forward, from Mark Wilkerson's "Run Mark Run" campaign to feed kids in Haiti to Chief Marketing Officer Brian Lauber's dedication and support of their local community. None of these shines as bright as it does when the company meets for its annual meetings. As a group who encourages and supports every employee to give back as individuals, few companies can say that they volunteer a work day to help feed the world. In the summer of 2011, in Colorado Spring, over 300 OneAmerica employees gave up a day of their vacation time to help support and feed over 100,000 people by creating meals for the Kids Around the World program.

"OneAmerica knows there are many organizations that claim to be in the financial services field, but those folks are usually in the financial processing business", explained Mark Glavin. "At OneAmerica, we are in the 'financial services' business because we are servants and that says it all."

Another great quote from CEO Dayton Molendorp is: "When someone shows you who they really are, believe them." With OneAmerica, it is easy to know who they are, and easy to believe them. They are Servants, who serve others by giving forward with a promise that they will always be there when you need them most.

CCCi—Where Technology Has a Heart

The CCCi story started one fateful day in the 1970's when Pat McBrayer, a respected IT consultant, became fed up with the way things worked. Troubled by the unethical business practices he witnessed in the IT industry, including his own résumé being misrepresented to a client without his knowledge, Pat decided there had to be a better way. So he struck out on his own and the rest, as they say, is history.

Pat and his wife, Charleen, were among the pioneers in the IT professional services industry when they launched a one-customer consulting business in Atlanta called Comprehensive Computer Consulting, Inc. in 1978, and that first customer is still a CCCi client today! Pat and Charleen grew CCCi from a company with one IT consultant to a thriving firm that today employs more than 400 IT professionals and serves a diverse and prestigious client base.

But that is just the beginning.

Putting people first is what they are all about.

Since day one, CCCi seemed to march to a different drummer, placing the value of people and relationships above all else. The dedication to building the business one relationship at a time and putting people first has survived the test of time and propelled CCCi's growth through even the most challenging economic times.

Upon Pat's passing in 1995, Charleen became CEO and held firm to Pat's vision of helping IT professionals and connecting customers with high-quality IT services. "I remember when it struck me after Pat's death that we not only had several hundred employees, but we had several hundred 'families,'" said Charleen. "And I was not about to let them down."

Guided by CCCi's principles and values, Charleen took the reins and has steadily grown the business into the premier IT professional services firm it is today, but in addition to hard work, Charleen and her team focus on the most precious principle of all, 'Giving Forward.'

Every day, somewhere in the country, a CCCi employee is giving ahead to their community, clients, and family. Whether it is a Donate Life Campaign for organ donors, participating in the Transplant Games, or washing kids feet and giving them new shoes through Samaritans Feet, CCCi is there, and they are serving with a passion.

"It is why we are here," said Charleen, "to serve others and hopefully support and provide them a better life."

CCCi has supplied over 10,000,000 hours of IT staff support, but that does not compare to the number of lives they have impacted across the country. That's what makes them special and a leader within the world's Top 1%, giving forward is not just an action, it is a life. It is who you are, and no one does it with the heart and soul of CCCi.

Technology really does have a heart.

About the Author

Donald W. Barden

To many, Don Barden is a classically trained economist who is fluent in international business affairs, but as he likes to say, "I am really a frustrated anthropologist!" Even though he loves to lecture and teach on world affairs and the economy, he is always quick to point out that he cares more about "why people make decisions," than he does about "yield curves and interest rates."

Don loves motivating people to think deeply about their beliefs. His "unfair advantage" theories are revolutionary in today's world. Don will lead you on a journey that exposes the myth of modern sales and marketing and identifies the pathway to consistent cultural change.

Expertly mixing humor and academic capital, Don engages audiences through his highly personal and interactive writing and speaking style. Don will shake your fundamental belief systems and reset your foundations with his unique ability to break down barriers and build an irresistible and motivated force that is focused on growth and the future.

As an author, speaker, advisor and corporate executive, Don Barden's counsel is highly sought after by some of the world's most successful businesses. His experience and record-setting sales success have drawn him to corporate and political leaders who want to tap into his real-world experience in order to move their organization to higher levels of achievement. Don has personally worked with some of the world's best known brands and has reshaped the production landscape of 3 major financial institutions. He has personally averaged over $1billion a year in annual asset sales.

He has doctoral studies in Behavioral Finance with an M.B.A. in Global Technology Management and International Business as well as an undergraduate B.B.A. in Economics and Finance.

Don is currently the Board Chairman of the Summit Counseling Center in Atlanta—a multi-disciplined facility delivering over 6,000 clinical hours of therapy per year, and a passionate supporter of the 1st Ranger Battalion stationed at Hunter Airfield in Savannah, Georgia.

Special Thanks to everyone who contributed over the years ...

Lisa, Jake, Luke, and Nick for your love and patience!

Bruce Marciano, John Maxwell, Ravi Zacharias, Allen Hunt, David and Vicki Smith, and all of the Doctors, Counselors' and staff at the Summit Counseling Center, for the life changing moments.

Mike Kaplan, Casey Jones III, Neal Howard, and Rick Swerdlin

Dave Bigler, John Pickard, Patrick Barry, Mike Voegele, Tom Nicol, Don Weitzel, Scott Fenstermaker, Scott Fjeldstad, Mike Robinson, and Robb Hill.

Scott Keller CFA, Gene Henssler PhD, Ted Parrish CFA, Retired U.S. Navy Cmdr. Michael S. Quinlan, and William Lako CFP.

George Castineiras, C. Robert Henrikson, Robert BenMosche, William Toppeta, Tim Mitchell, Brian J Fox, Robert Merck, William Wheeler, Maria Morris, Larry Karl and John Morabito

Fred Castellani, George Sutherland, Jim Gilligan, Scott Pawlitch, Tanya Jones, Palmer Whitney, Bill Feldmeir, Shefali Desai, Sarah Elliott, and with special memories to Robert Cunningham.

Dayton Molendorp, Mark Roller, Brian Lauber, Mark Wilkerson, Bill Yoerger, Mark Glavin, Marsha Whitehead, Angela Trefethen, Mitch Haber, Ana Etcheverry, and Eric Pete.

Kyle Lenard, Erin Mitchell, Scott Brown, Alice Davis and Brittany Behn

Burke Robinson, George Norton, Fred Erler, Ron Murray, Fritz Scheffel, Anthony Walsh, Noland Deas, Kirk Somers, Steven Deaton, Jim Milar, Phillip and Robin McEuen

Alex and Louisa Grigorian, Bill Mitchell, Rob Mimms, Jeff Frantz, Mike and Jennifer Walley, Andy and Barb Scott, The Kanemasu's, The Hunt's, The Fischer's, The Brown's, The Cobia's, The Antin's, The Wachowiak's, Solomon Gizaw, and the entire Ellard Community

Indiana, Kansas, Canada, as well as the UK, Italy, Czech Republic, Germany, France, Mexico, India, Brazil, Peru, Indonesia, Costa Rica, Belize, Panama, Australia, New Zealand, and Japan.

Greg Baker

Pamela Harty and everyone at The Knight Agency

To all of the test subjects, organizations, and company's around the world that let us into their lives only for us to discover that our hearts were changed by your service to us and others, we thank you.

For more information on The Perfect Plan with updates of people and organizations that make up the Elite 1 %, visit our website at:

www.theperfectplantoday.com

You can also follow us on Facebook, Linkedin, Twitter and YouTube

Don Barden can be reached at donbarden@theperfectplantoday.com

Jeremiah 29:11
New International Version (NIV)

"For I know the plans I have for you," declares the Lord, "plans to prosper you and not to harm you, plans to give you hope and a future."

Made in the USA
Middletown, DE
11 November 2014